WHO'S GONNA FIX YOUR CAR NOW?

WHO'S GONNA FIX YOUR CAR NOW?

THE MECHANIC SHORTAGE: THE CAUSE AND THE CURE

Tom Fennell

WEESEE, INC.
Geneva, Illinois

First printing 2000

ISBN 0-9671099-4-9

LCCN 99-95067

Contents

Acknowledgments

The last thing you want is to sound cliche when it comes to thanking your wife and family and so on. But my wife Cindy, my daughter Colleen, and my son Sean have been great about understanding why I have spent so much time in my office recently. During the first several months of writing this book, I was also finishing a manuscript about my life to leave to my children and grandchildren. I was home so seldom, they practically needed an appointment to see me. I owe them a great deal of thanks.

To my niece Jennifer and two of my nephews Colm and Peter—their help with reviewing and retyping was invaluable. To all the mechanics, service managers, and parts managers who filled out the surveys or allowed me to interview them—my sincere thanks. Thanks, too, for the input from some of my workmates and friends.

Everything will have been worthwhile if this book helps to bring about the changes that make being a mechanic a desirable trade again. This will take a serious commitment from the manufacturers and dealers; it can and must be done.

Introduction

How much do you know about the development of the automobile? The reason for this book is not to attempt to make you an expert on the history of the auto or a technical wizard. My purpose is to explain, from an insider's view, the changes that have taken place over the years that, according to industry statistics, have caused a shortage of 60,000 mechanics a year. This is a cumulative number of those leaving the profession and the lack of people coming into the profession, which will effect the quality of the repairs you can expect when your car has a problem.

Who will fix the problem and what training do these people have? Since my background is entirely with European and Japanese manufacturers, my opinion does not cover all manufacturers. But as my father would have said, "If the devil was a barber he would have a hard time shaving the difference."

I began a mechanic apprenticeship as a 13-year-old in Dublin, Ireland, where I was born. There, as in most European countries, the apprenticeship program consists of two nights a week of theory and one full day a week of workshop in the college of technology. During this time, I worked as an apprentice to a mechanic in a dealership. If you pass the tests at the end of the four-year program, the government certifies you as a mechanic.

I emigrated to America on a sponsored program through an employment agency. I worked for a year in Georgia and then a year in Florida as an import car mechanic. Then I got a break and became a service rep for a European manufacturer; my territory covered 14 states and 120 dealers. I resigned that position to become a service manager at an import dealership in Illinois. Following four years as a service manager, I went back to the wholesale side of the business working for an independent distributor of a Japanese car. There I spent three years as a district manager followed by three years as the distributor manager. As the distributor manager I was responsible for the district service managers and the customer relations, warranty, and technical training departments. I will discuss independent distributors later in the book. I spent the next six years as a district service and parts manager for yet another Japanese product covering some of the midwestern states.

I left that position to work in a joint venture factory (Japanese-American) as a quality assurance manager. Health and other reasons caused me to resign this position, and I have been in my current position as a technical specialist for a European manufacturer covering nine Midwest states for nine years.

What Is the Issue?

It all started back about 40 years ago, when I told my mother I wanted to be a mechanic. Her disappointment was obvious and centered around the stigma that the occupation of a mechanic is a dirty, greasy trade—not at all what she wanted for her son. She told me several times that she wanted me to be a white-collar worker. I was never able to explain to her that although our hands and coveralls were dirty, we did have to use our brains a lot.

There were two incidents that happened years ago that made me realize people's perceptions about mechanics. When I first determined that I wanted to be a mechanic, my father said it would be best if I went to work for a friend of his who owned a repair shop next to our house. The repair shop was a corrugated shed that had originally been built for cockfighting. (I am happy to say I have never seen a cockfight.) It was a dirty place to work and cleaning your hands was a matter of washing them in a bucket of paraffin oil in which you had just washed a transmission.

One of the mechanics sent me to the store for him once. When I handed the note to the storekeeper, a customer commented about how dirty the note was and how dirty mechanics were. The shopkeeper told the woman the money might be dirty but it was hard-earned and my business was appreciated.

Another time, I was working at a large dealership with at least 30 mechanics. There was an office staff there of at least a half dozen females, some of whom were quite attractive. Naturally, I tried to make friends with one of them. When the big boss found out, I was called into his office and informed that mechanics were to have no contact with office staff. I admit, I was hurt.

Although cars have changed and the role of the mechanic has changed from a nuts-and-bolts worker to a highly educated, computer-literate professional, this new role of the mechanic is not well known outside the profession and it's causing an image problem. The grease-monkey stigma still exists. The industry as a whole has attempted to change this by using the term technician rather than mechanic; but frankly, when it comes to diagnosing problems on modern cars, "wizard" might be more appropriate.

When I was young it seemed that most guys my age loved cars and speed; we were often referred to as "gear heads." A lot of us became mechanics so we could afford to own and repair our own cars. Today, most teens are into computers and stereos, so there is very little new blood coming into the car business. Certainly, there are other reasons why we can't attract young men into the business—flat-rate pay, warranty work, and unreasonable customers, to name a few. Others include dealer principals who treat mechanics with less respect than they deserve, service managers who are difficult to deal with, and last—but not least—factory people and factory-required tests.

Even the young "gear heads" of today are going to work for independent, nonfactory-authorized repair shops rather than dealerships. I'm not referring to the chains that service tires, batteries, and exhaust systems but the true independent repair shops. There are still quite a few of them, but they are a dying breed. Some of the reasons they are struggling to make it are the cost of the equipment to perform diagnoses, the cost of special tools to perform the repairs, and the lack of technical information.

Yes, they can get copies of service bulletins, but they cannot send a mechanic to a factory-conducted technical training class. This is in fact a double loss because although the mechanic may be there for an electrical class, there is so much chitchat among the mechanics at these schools, they pick up a lot of information about other problems, either from the training instructor or the other mechanics. There is a great sharing of information that goes on at these technical classes that cannot be found in any service bulletin.

If a mechanic working for an independent has, say, a drive ability problem on a 1992 car, to whom can he turn for help? If one of the other mechanics cannot help him, he guesses; this can get very expensive for the customer. Electronic and electrical parts are nonreturnable, so if the part he ordered does not fix the problem, he has to sell the customer on the idea that it would have needed replacing soon anyway.

Given the same situation in a dealership, the mechanic has several options. He can call the district service manager. If he doesn't have the answer, the mechanic can call the factory technical hotline. If the problem is such that it can't be resolved without personnel involvement, they will give advice and make an appointment for a technical specialist to visit the dealer. Because dealerships have these types of advantages and because cars are becoming more technologically advanced with the diagnostic equipment more expensive and the training more specialized, how long can the independents stay in business?

In spite of the advantages of dealerships, many mechanics prefer working for independents for various reasons. Often mechanics get paid more per hour since the independent's overhead is much less than a dealership's. Because the independents do not perform warranty work, the owners are generally more service-oriented, which increases the respect factor for mechanics.

Since we are talking about independent repair shops, I'd like to share a story about a friend of mine. He is the author of a book called *The Last Open Road.* He and I became friends when we were both racing cars. The main thing we had in common was that we were always broke. I had the advantage of being a mechanic so I could do all the work on my car myself; but he had to pay mechanics to work on his car, which he could not afford. So he came up with a great idea: He would open his own repair shop. That way, he could make money *and* have mechanics available to work on his race car.

He borrowed as much money as he could, found a shop in the city, hired two mechanics, sent out flyers, and organized a huge grand opening. He had no idea how many friends he had until the party—there must have been a couple hundred people who showed up. The party left him so broke, the business never got off the ground. The moral of this story is not to have the party until the business is up and running.

Would it hurt or help the dealers if there were no independent repair shops around? The most important reason it would hurt is that the independents are competition for the dealer and competition displaces complacency so the customer wins. In addition, there are customers who are not comfortable with taking their car to the dealer. Some people also think the dealer will be more expensive than the independent, which is not necessarily true. Others feel they have a closer relationship with the independent. Plus, the independents are generally good customers for the dealers parts department.

Pay

Can a mechanic make a good living? Yes, he can; however, there are many variables. His tools are of course his most important asset and a large expense, averaging between $35,000 and $45,000. Most mechanics have a running account with the tool salesman that they pay money on every week, either to upgrade or maintain the quality of their tools.

There are several different ways mechanics get paid, but the most common are straight salary or flat rate. Straight salary is self-explanatory. Flat rate, however, can be confusing. For example, someone brings a car in for service and waits for the repair to be completed. What often happens is that the person receives a bill for two hours labor when in fact the mechanic only worked on the car for an hour and a half. The idea of the flat rate system is that the manufacturers set a time on every repair. These repair times are established in a repair shop at the factory and the time that ends up in the flat rate book is an average of the time it took the repair to be performed three times. If a mechanic replaces a transmission and the flat rate time is four hours but he completes the job in three, he is paid the full four hours. But, if it takes him five hours, he only gets paid for four. The major problem for the mechanic is a car with a difficult electrical problem. Most factories only pay a limited amount of time for diagnosis, so a mechanic might spend all day trying to find a problem and only get paid two hours.

I can speak from personal experience on this: I once worked all day on a car with an electrical problem and finally discovered a faulty switch was responsible. I was paid just two tenths of an hour to replace this switch.

On another occasion, a factory rep visited our shop and came over to talk to me just as I began to overhaul a transmission. He chatted for the two hours it took me to complete the job. When I was finished, he pointed out that bench time for that job was four hours and I did it in two. I said that was the idea behind the flat rate. Several weeks later his company issued a service bulletin changing the bench time for that transmission to two hours. I was not a happy camper. He had the nerve to call me a few weeks later to find out if I was having a problem with the idle on a new car.

I said I was, and he asked if I'd figured out how to fix it. I said I had, but when he asked me to share what I'd learned with him, I shared only a few choice words before I hung up on him.

It's important to mention at this point that although the dealer's labor charge may be \$65 per hour, the average pay for a mechanic is about \$16 per hour. The difference is what the dealer needs to cover overhead costs, such as rent, insurance, utilities, and profits.

What happens in the case of a comeback? It depends on the problem. The service manager or the shop foreman will review the situation to make that decision. If it is determined that this problem was not related to the original problem, one of three things will happen. If the car is within the warranty period, there will be a warranty claim against the factory for the new repair. If the repair is not the same as what the car came in for and it's a customer pay repair, that is more awkward. Generally, when I was a service manager, I would take the customer to the car so that I could show him or her the parts involved and try to explain the repair. If the customer did not understand, I would try to negotiate. Statistics tell us that if you can keep a customer you will make hundreds of thousands of dollars over his or her lifetime of ownership. It's important to keep this in mind, along with the customer's history with your dealership.

What if a mechanic caused the comeback? Normally, the mechanic will do the repair again for free, although the dealership will eat the cost of the parts. If it is the second or more time the same mechanic has had a comeback, he may be sent home for a day or some other punishment may given to make him more careful in the future.

Recently, I visited a dealer to resolve a problem and observed a discussion between the shop foreman and a mechanic about a comeback. In this case, the shop foreman actually made the comeback repair for a heater motor the mechanic had installed two days previously that now did not work. The shop foreman pulled the center consul and connected a wire properly the mechanic had left loose; the repair took about fifteen minutes. Since I was working on this book, I followed up to find out what the consequence was for the mechanic. In this particular dealership, mechanics are paid $16 per hour. If, at the end of a month, they have turned at least 160 hours and have no comebacks, their pay will be $18 per hour retroactive to the first hour. If they have one comeback they will get $17.50; two comebacks drops them to $17 per hour; three comebacks and they are paid the straight $16 per hour for this month. Comebacks hurt everyone—the mechanic, the dealer, and of course, the customer.

Some shops have what is known as a team system. Each team consists of three or five mechanics of decreasing ability. The idea is that the low man does the basic work such as brakes, exhaust, and shocks; the next man does tune-ups; and the top man is the diagnostic man (top dog). It seems like a good idea, but there are problems with it. If the top two mechanics like their jobs, what does the bottom man do after a year or so when he is ready to move up? He has to leave and find another job. A shop set up in teams of equally qualified mechanics does work. In fact, if a shop has more than ten mechanics I recommend it.

Productivity and Efficiency

There are several ways in which mechanics' abilities are measured. The oldest methods are *productivity* and *efficiency*. Let me explain productivity first. If a mechanic clocks in at 8:00 AM and takes an hour-long lunch break and two quarter-hour breaks, then clocks out at 5:30 PM, that is an eight-hour shift. Each time he completes a job, he has to clock on and off the job; if, at the end of the day, his total time clocked on jobs is six hours, his productivity would be 80% . What happened to the other 20%? That is what the service manager must find out. The two most common reasons are too much time waiting at the parts counter or too much time waiting for the dispatcher or service manager to assign the next job.

Efficiency is the difference between clocked on time and flat rate time. If a mechanic works on four cars in an eight-hour day and the combined flat (factory allowed time) for those jobs is 10 hours, he is 116% efficient. Conversely, if the flat rate time for those combined jobs was six hours; he would be 84% efficient. Consequently, the best and most efficient mechanic gets stuck with all the difficult jobs. Fair? Of course not, but that is the way it works in most shops; it then becomes the service manager's job to compensate the mechanic. The service manager feeds him some "gravy work" (no-brainer projects such as brake jobs, exhaust work, and maintenance) to make up for the time he lost on the difficult job. It is easy for most mechanics to beat the flat rate on these types of jobs. With a good service manager, the hours will balance out most of the time. If not, the mechanic will generally tell the service manager that if the hours don't balance out, he may quit. If the service manager is smart, he will make sure it is right, because it's too hard to find a good replacement.

In many of these situations, the service manager will make the top mechanic a salaried employee to avoid extra paperwork and bookkeeping, and this works well in many cases. However, many of these situations depend on the size of the dealership and what the franchise is. The size of the dealership matters because it's simply easier to manage a 3-man shop than a 20-man shop. The franchise makes a difference because some manufacturers are much more liberal than others when it comes to paying for diagnostic time and straight time; some have more direct accessibility to technical information and help.

Most mechanics prefer to stay with a certain brand of car and it may well be there is only one dealer in a 100-mile radius. If they quit a particular dealer, they would have to work on some other brand. It is also likely that if the mechanic has been around for a few years, he has built a loyal customer base, which almost guarantees work even during slow times.

Another reason for brand loyalty is that mechanics most likely have been to most if not all of the training schools for a particular brand and would hate to have to start over with another brand. In fact, if a mechanic has achieved a master technician rating with a brand, it is usually worth a little more money per hour of pay. If you recall how the flat rate method works, familiarity with and training on a brand is the best way to increase efficiency. Also, mechanics have likely invested in many tools specific to a particular brand which have no use on another brand.

What happens if no work or at least not enough work comes into the shop for the mechanic to make money? If the mechanic is a salaried employee, he gets his regular pay; if he is a flat rate mechanic, he is usually guaranteed about 30 hours pay, although this varies from dealer to dealer. Back when I last twisted wrenches for a living I was paid 50/50; in other words, if the labor charge was $40 per hour, regardless of who was paying the bill (the factory or the customer), I was paid $20 per hour. I had a guarantee of $100 per week. Things have changed now, with the average labor charge now about $70 per hour and the average mechanic being paid about $16 per hour. I even quit one dealer when we had two very slow weeks and they couldn't afford to give me the guarantee. By the following Monday, I was working for another import dealer in town.

Is there a difference between customer pay and warranty work? Yes. Flat rate times are developed by the factory to be fair compensation for work performed during the warranty period to ensure the satisfaction of their customers. Warranty work was never intended to be a profit center for the dealer. There are many companies that sell the dealers flat rate manuals that are designed to be fair to the customer and the mechanic. The two most popular are Chilton and Mitchell. On average they are about 20% more generous than the factory books, so although the customer is certainly not being cheated, you can see why the mechanic would prefer to work on customer pay repairs. Dealerships would also prefer customer work for several reasons. When a warranty repair is complete a claim has to be submitted to the factory, which is extra paper work, and in most busy dealerships this requires a full-time warranty person. In a high percentage of the repairs there is diagnostic time involved or straight time. There are so many things that can happen to a car, that the flat rate book can't cover every conceivable type of repair; so if the repair made is not in the book, they straight-time it.

In these cases, the service manager has to contact the district manager to get an authorization to submit the claim. Whether he gets approval for the full amount or not depends on several issues. For example, how experienced is the district manager? How much does he trust the dealer? How much pressure is he under to watch expenses. At regional meetings, regional managers will show overheads of current warranty expenses to district managers, giving them a subtle or not-so-subtle message. Subsequently, the district manager goes back into the field, afraid to authorize anything without negotiating it down to the least possible amount with the service manager.

Ten or 15 years ago, all district managers were technically oriented and had backgrounds as mechanics or service managers, which gave the dealer service manager a certain comfort level. In 1982, the company I went to work for insisted on all district managers having at least three years as a service manager, three years as a mechanic, and some experience as a district manager with another manufacturer.

In the past 15 years or so, most of the manufacturers began hiring college graduates for the position of district manager, adding technical specialists to each area and a national technical hot line. This arrangement allows the district manager the time to keep closer tabs on warranty costs, financial statement analysis, and customer service. The problem service managers have is that they find it difficult to explain to a nontechnical person why a problem was so hard to find when they need an authorization for diagnostic time.

Most service managers would prefer the old days when the district managers had a technical background, although from the factory point of view the current system works well. The nontechnical guys seem to be a lot better at reporting or documenting, and since they were never mechanics they don't have the same feeling for a mechanic when they disallow time spent on a repair.

How Honest Are Mechanics and Dealers?

This is probably the question I have been asked most over the past 30 years or so by people who know I am in the car business. The fact is, you could ask the same question about any business or trade and the answer would be the same: Most of them are honest. But how do you know which ones? As with any other service, word of mouth is generally the best measure.

Let me tell a few stories about dishonest mechanics and the consequences of their actions. During a dealer visit I asked the service manager about a part a mechanic said he had replaced to do a warranty repair but which we could not find in the warranty bins. The service manager said it must still be on the mechanic's bench. The mechanic in question was out on a test drive, so we looked all over his bench, but could not find the part. Since the mechanic's tool box was open we looked in the bottom part of his box where we found many new parts. Why would there be new parts in his toolbox? Because he had charged them out to customer or warranty repair orders and never installed them. This mechanic was fired immediately upon returning to the dealer. All mechanics were then told to open their toolboxes for inspection. I am happy to report no other dishonest mechanic was found.

My second story occurred while I was teaching a technical update class some years ago. One mechanic interrupted constantly, telling stories about how he cheated customers. I finally told him to get out of the class. The following day, I called the service manager and the general manager of the dealership where the mechanic worked to describe what had happened. They never allowed him to attend any other schools, which in fact I had no control over since I was not the technical training instructor. But the end result was that he never went back to a school and eventually had to leave the dealership.

The third story takes place at a dealership I had visited several times but was not impressed with their ability to repair cars. Each time I went there, the mechanics did not follow proper diagnostic procedures. In each case, it was a different mechanic but in the course of working with them to fix these cars, they both told me how great this dealership was to work at and told me how much money they were averaging per week. My first reaction was how could they be such poor mechanics and make this kind of money? Eventually, I found the answer when a new mechanic was hired. This mechanic was not only a good mechanic, but an honest one. In the course of working beside the other two mechanics, he discovered they were installing unnecessary parts on cars. He reported this action to the service director, which resulted in them both being fired. This mechanic also informed our district manager, who requested the warranty audit team to come to the dealership, which as you can imagine was very expensive. Thanks to the honesty of one mechanic, neither of those dishonest guys has worked in a dealership since. I hear they started their own independent repair shop. I hope they are out of business by now.

I will tell one more story because it goes to the root of what this book is about. What happened in this case the mechanic was given a routine service to do on a customer car, just an oil and filter change. He turned in the ticket and the customer paid his bill and left; however, the customer came back a short time later and pointed out to the service writer a mark he had made on his original filter that was still there. The new oil filter was found in the mechanic's toolbox.

There are two things that are very disturbing about this: first, I had worked with this mechanic on some problem cars when I covered a different area and thought he was a very nice young man. The second issue—and the most disturbing—is that this mechanic was working for one of the other dealers in town within a day. Of course, they had full knowledge of what had happened but they were so desperate for mechanics they were prepared to take the chance. Undoubtedly, he will be under observation by the managers and the other mechanics because they are concerned about the reputation of the dealership. Any loss of customers affects them also.

What about the honesty of dealers themselves? That is a bit more complicated. A high percentage of dealerships are run by a general manager because many dealer principals have more than one store and are not too involved in day-to-day store operations. Even those that do not have more than one store are busy with other things such as advertising and committees with the franchise or franchises they sell. Most dealer principals see the service department as a necessary evil. They would prefer to have nothing to do with the service department.

Because I have called on dealerships for so many years, there aren't too many rumors about dishonest dealers I haven't heard. In more than 30 years of calling on dealers, I was only approached by one general manager requesting that I be part of a scam. I had told the service manager that this would be the last time I would call on him because I had given the company two weeks notice that I was leaving. About an hour later the general manager called me into his office and asked why I was leaving. I said the company did not pay well enough. He asked how much it would take for me to stay. I told him $600 a month.

He instructed me to call my boss and tell him I was staying because he would mail a $600 check to my home each month. Of course, I refused and reported the incident to the company. He must have had friends in high places, however, because not only did he not get fired, he became the dealer principal.

Some years ago I was talking to the owner of a dealership in his office when the sales rep from their other franchise came in. That brand of car was very hard to get at the time, so the dealer asked the rep what it would take to get ten cars. The rep said, "I am having central air installed in my house and it will cost $1,200." The dealer told the rep to send him the bill for the air-conditioning. Apparently, this rep was not the only one from that company doing this and eventually it ended up in court and some people went to jail. But these are the exceptions to the rule on both the factory and the dealer side, I am happy to say.

I have interviewed many service managers about their job, pay, and relationships with general managers. Overall, they don't feel they are getting a fair shake. In many cases, the general manager changed their bonus, commission, benefits, or all of the above, and they will not do as well next year as they did the previous year. I even had some sales managers tell me the same story

On the one hand they need the people in the back end (parts and service) to be satisfied because that is where they make their money; on the other hand, it may be the only place they can cut costs. This puts them right between the dog and the hydrant, so to speak. The back end pays the major portion of the total overheads of the dealership and yet it's about the only place they can do cost cutting. Was it always this way? No. So what changed? I will use the words of a sales manager to try to explain.

I had just finished a product presentation at a dealership and went outside to have a cigarette. Three or four sales people joined me. Because I was the factory guy, they complained to me about how little money they made on our product. I said, "Well, how much do you make with the other brands you sell?"

They agreed it was about the same. I asked if they thought it was the factories that controlled how much they made on a car. The manager, who was about my age—55 or so—said to the others, who were in their thirties, "We did it to ourselves." I told him to explain to the others what he meant. He said that about 20 or more years ago sales were slow and some salesman got the idea to show the customers the actual invoice of the car to prove how close to the bone he was cutting the deal. It did not take long for this to be so common, dealers were not making enough money to keep the doors open. Then the factories had to jump in and help the dealers by putting in place a type of bonus the dealer got and still does for each car sold. You can well imagine that is when the entire profit structure of the dealerships changed; up to that point the front end covered the major portion of the overheads and the back end made the difference plus profit.

So parts and labor charges had to be jacked up to increase the profitability, but the mechanic's pay did not increase. Now the mechanic went from a 50/50 split of the labor charge to getting less than 25% of the labor charge. This is when *the flat rate system died and should have been buried but was not.*

So, here we are, 20-some years later and it is common practice for dealers to show the actual invoice to customers. I heard a radio spot recently for a large domestic dealer that said they would sell any car for $7 over invoice. You can log on to the Internet to see how much a dealer paid for a car. Is that a bad thing? Yes. Can something be done to change this? You can't find out what your house cost the builder to build or how much profit the company made that sold you your refrigerator or television. I know of least one American manufacturer that was pursuing the idea that the invoice to the dealers should be a legal document and not available to salesmen or anyone else. I hope a resolution is found. Until that happens, the dealer principals or general managers have little choice but to keep a tight reign on the salaries and other expenses in the service and parts departments.

Earlier I explained that it is difficult to attract young people into being mechanics. Let me give you a few examples of what I mean. In the last five years or so, at least two manufacturers I am aware of have developed a reward system for their dealers based on the customer satisfaction index (CSI). If the dealership maintains a certain level of satisfaction in all departments as measured by surveys, the factory will reward them with a sizeable amount of money to be shared among all the employees. This is the way it should be. It takes a great effort on the part of every employee to bring customer satisfaction up to that level.

There was, however, one difference in the two manufacturers' programs. In one case, the dealers had to sign a form agreeing to how the money would be divided. In the other, when the program was introduced, how the money was to be divided was just a verbal recommendation. So as you might suspect, not all dealers that received money have shared it with the back-end employees. I am not sure if the sales people got any money or not. In some instances, the dealer set additional goals the mechanics have to achieve to receive any money. One dealer with several franchises in the same building decided to share the money with the entire staff, including the porters, which is fine except that the porters received a greater amount than the mechanics. The general manager's explanation was that the porters have more contact with the customers than the mechanics. It comes as no surprise that the mechanics' attitude has become "let the porters fix the cars" and the dealership has never made it into the money since. Although they are technically not doing anything wrong, it sure is shortsighted. As far as the mechanics are concerned, it's not so much the money; it's the meaning and it hurts.

You may think I am picking on dealers of one or two franchise just because I am familiar with them, but remember a high percentage of these dealers own a lot of other franchises.

I understand that although the other franchises reward them in different ways, if it was a cash reward from their other franchises, the results would be the same. Although this is a small percentage of dealers, one with this attitude is too many. Among the dealers that do share the money, one of the most inventive plans I have heard about is where the service manager reviews each job with the mechanics and pays them however much time they have in the job. For example, if the flat rate for a job is four hours and the mechanic takes six hours, he is paid for six hours. At the end of the quarter when the payout is calculated, the service manager converts the dollars to hours and if a mechanic received 20 additional hours during the quarter then that amount is deducted from his bonus amount. It does require some additional bookkeeping, but the mechanics like it and the dealership is consistently in the money, so it works. The customers are happy and that is the goal.

Are dealers honest? Well, in general they are; I just have a problem with most of their attitudes when it comes to the people in the back end. It reminds me of when I was in Japan for training and I was invited to my boss's house for dinner. I had made it clear that I would not eat raw fish, so his wife made a special effort to prepare American food for me. It was very good, so I told my boss to thank his wife for me. He said he would not because it was her job.

The Customer: Know Your Rights, Know Your Car

Let's take a break from all that dealer mechanic stuff and talk about you, the customer. Are all customers nice? It makes no difference what business you pick; if you deal with customers, you will meet the few who strive to make your life miserable. This chapter is for the 95% who are nice and a pleasure to deal with even when you are upset with the product. So I would like to talk about your rights and give you some tips on explaining problems to the service writers, as well as explain some of the equipment on your car and tell a few stories.

Lemon laws came into being about 10 years ago to give customers an avenue to resolve repeat repair problems. In fact, they work well for the factories also. Now that people are aware there are such laws, they at least call the customer relations department to review their options, which makes the factory aware of the problems a lot sooner than in the past. Does that mean you will get a new car? No, but it does mean that it will get fixed a lot sooner if there is a repair required; if not, then the factory will work something out with you. If it can't be worked out to your satisfaction, then you can pursue the matter with an attorney, though it usually doesn't go that far.

Here is an example of the basic parameters of a typical lemon law. (In this case, it's the Illinois law. This is not a direct quote from the law but gives some basic verbiage to explain what the law is about.) If a problem happens within the first 12 months or 12,000 miles and the dealer has made four attempts to fix the problem or if the car is in the shop for more than 30 days, the factory has one final repair attempt. The other basic parameters needed are that the problem greatly affects the safety, use, or market value of the car. I recommend that if after two attempts the car is not right, you should ask the service manager to contact the factory rep and explain your problem. I would also ask the service manager for the name of the person and a phone number in case you have to make direct contact. You may also check with your local Better Business Bureau to see if they have an arbitration arrangement with the manufacturer.

Buy-Backs

It always surprises me how many nonautomotive people ask me, "Do the factories really buy back cars?" Yes, under some circumstances. These are cars outside of the lemon law because within the boundaries of the lemon law there are criteria that must be met within a specified time limit. It is difficult to get a car bought back, even if there are legitimate reasons. Let me explain.

Some years ago I was sitting in the service manager's office of a dealership that had three franchises. The service manager came into his office followed by a man with a check in his hand and a big smile on his face. He asked the service manager, "Do you know what was wrong with my truck?"

"No," answered the service manager, "we were never able to make it do what you said it does." The man told him there was never anything wrong with the truck. He just couldn't afford the payments because he was out of work. He had no job but plenty of time to hound the service manager and the factory until they agreed to buy it back.

On one occasion I met an attorney who claimed he had a severe shake in his steering at 120 miles per hour and was hounding the customer relation's people and the service rep. So, of course, they dumped it on the technical guy (me). When I looked at the car, I told the customer and the service manager the car had after-market wheels. The customer said he had the shake before he put on the after-market wheels; the service manager said he had balanced the wheels several times. I knew there was only one way to find out if there was a problem.

I took the car out on the interstate and took it up to 120. It shook like all heck. I went back to the dealership and had them install the wheels from my car onto the customer's car and repeated the test. There was no shake. Why did the customer lie? Well, he wanted to be upgraded to a current year model car and figured we would just accept his story.

I have met with people who were demanding buy-backs for everything from bad radio reception to a bad or erratic temperature gauge to shakes, rattles, brake noises, and on and on. Some have been successful in either getting the car bought back or getting some money to help upgrade to a newer model. In some cases, I have seen the factory give the customer a check and request it be used toward the cost of trading the car for some other brand. (In other words, please don't buy our product again.) I have had some customers tell me they have had more than one factory buy cars back in the past. So for some it's a challenge or a game. Some just lie about a problem because they can no longer afford the payments or they are going to exceed the mileage limit on a lease. Unfortunately, the cost of buy-backs is added to the price structure of next-year models.

Because of these types of people, factories are gun shy about any request for a buy-back or assistance to upgrade to a newer model. The factories do want to help people with legitimate problems, but be prepared to jump through hoops if you request a buy-back.

Repairs

When you bring your car in for a repair it is very important to give as much detail as possible to the person writing the order. For example, try to provide the following information:

- What is the ambient temperature?
- What type of road will make it happen?
- Does it happen when the brakes are applied?
- Was the car in an accident?

If you are back for the second time with a noise, insist the mechanic go for a ride with you. It will save a lot of frustration.

If it is an electrical problem that blows fuses, try to establish when it happens. For example:

- When you turn on the radio?
- When you use the turn signals?
- When you use the brakes?

Again, it is extremely important to give the mechanic every piece of information you can. For example, recently I was requested to visit a dealership to inspect a car that was in for the third or fourth time with a starting problem. When I reviewed the repair history, all of the past repair orders and the new one stated, "Car would not start. Towed in." As I reviewed what repairs had been made, it seemed that every part related to the starting system had been replaced. I asked the service manager if he could get the customer on the phone so I could get more information. When I asked the customer if the car cranked but did not start or if it did not crank at all, she said the latter was the case. Because this critical piece of information was not on the repair order, the mechanics had been looking at all the wrong parts. Now that we knew the actual problem, it took only a few minutes to test the right parts and discover the safety neutral switch was the culprit.

One of the questions I am asked a lot, especially by friends and relatives, is should I buy an extended warranty? Well, if you plan to keep the car longer than the power train warranty the answer is yes. You may well be able to afford mufflers, brakes, shocks, and so on, but if you have a major engine problem you could be looking at $6,000 to $36,000 of repairs, depending on the make of car. The thing you need to check on before you buy an extended warranty is that it is backed by the manufacturer.

Now let's discuss some of the features on cars that raise a lot of questions among consumers.

Brakes

One of the most common questions in the car business is, "Why do my brakes squeal?" What our ears hear as a squeal is in fact a vibration between the brake pad and the piston that pushes the pad against the disc or rotor. If you know how the brakes on a bicycle work, disc brakes work on the same principal: The disc runs between two pads and when the brakes are applied, the pads squeeze on the disc. Like the rubber blocks grab the bicycle wheel, when you hear a squeal it is caused by a shine or glaze on the disc, which is generally caused by long light braking. I am not suggesting you wait until the last minute and slam on the brakes, but it's best to approach a stop light or stop sign with your foot lightly on the brake pedal for the last 30 yards rather than cruising that way for a hundred yards.

Some other reasons for squealing brakes are pad material and the correct paste or shim between the pad and the piston. The material in the pad has to withstand great heat and have good wear characteristics.

People often ask me what the difference is between standard and anti-lock brakes. The main purpose of the anti-lock braking system (ABS) is to prevent the wheels from locking. You cannot steer the car with the wheels locked up. Two misconceptions about ABS is that you can stop better on ice and that you can stop in a shorter distance. Both of these statements are false. The stopping distance is about the same, although it is safer because you can steer the car.

The reason you feel the pedal move under your foot when the ABS system is working is that each wheel has a sensor that measures the speed at which each wheel is turning. Imagine the wheel as one of those wheels in a casino that they spin and the piece of cardboard clicks over the pins as it turns. The piece of cardboard would be the sensor measuring the speed of the wheel and sending the information back to the computer. The computer is receiving the information from all four wheels and it applies or releases the brakes so you don't lock up a wheel. Once you have applied the brakes do not take your foot off the pedal again unless you have stopped the car or have finished braking.

What if the ABS system fails? Your car will simply revert back to standard brakes. Any type of failure will turn on the warning lamp on the dash, so you should check to make sure the brakes feel okay and call your dealer for an appointment.

Tires

Back in the mid-1970s, the Sports Car Club of America (SCCA) introduced a special racing class for showroom stock cars. The idea was that the car must not be modified in any way except to add the safety equipment (roll bar, six-point seatbelts, window net, and so on). Once it became a national class, however, the factories became involved, which meant money was involved. I will not say we were cheating—between you and me, of course we were!—but the cars were very much faster than those you could buy off the showroom floor. Back then, 70 series tires were the standard issue on cars and worked well under most conditions. Unfortunately, they did not withstand the heat of high-speed cornering very well, so there were a lot of bad accidents caused by tires coming apart. Finally, the tire manufacturers became involved and began manufacturing tires that did hold up.

Then came the low-profile tires and many other improvements that most likely would have happened without racing. But I believe it happened sooner rather than later because of racing.

Today there is a great selection of tires to choose from, but there are a few things to be aware of. First, do not mix and match. Use the same brand, size, and tread style on all four corners or your car may feel wishy-washy in turns. If you have a four-wheel drive or all-wheel drive, you will damage your transmission if you mix tires.

What about low profile tires like 40, 45, or 50 series tires? They look and handle great, but if you live in the Midwest or any place in the country where the snow is replaced by potholes every spring, it can get very expensive. If you live in a mild climate these tires are great, but they do give you a harsh ride, so before you order a car with these tires be sure to test drive a car with "rubber bands," as they are called, installed.

Supplemental Restraint System (SRS)

Your seatbelt is your main restraint and the SRS is just what it says, supplemental. I'll risk sounding like I'm preaching and say that seatbelts should be worn at all times. In one of my jobs, I was responsible for the crash-testing program and I got to see first hand the various types of crashes and the injuries they cause.

In my current position, I am responsible for investigating any accident that occurs in my territory when the driver claims the product did not perform as expected. By far, inspections involving air bag deployment or nondeployment are the most common.

What is the reason for the air bag? To save your face from being rearranged by the steering wheel in a front or front angular crash. You will always move in the direction of the impact. The crash sensor or sensors make the decision to deploy or not between 25 milliseconds and 125 milliseconds. Regardless of how bad the damage to the car looks, if the driver's face did not hit the steering wheel, the impact was not frontal enough and deployment was not called for.

If the bag did not deploy but there is a secondary impact, that is frontal, and meets the rate of deceleration required by the crash sensor, the bag will deploy. Another situation that causes questions is when there is little visible damage on the car but the bag deployed. This is much more difficult to explain, so I will just give you an idea of what happens. The crash sensor measures in two ways: time and deceleration rate. On newer cars with the big poly-filled bumpers or bumper shocks, the bumper can be pushed back hard enough to bottom against the frame rail. The combination of the bottoming against the frame and the increased time it takes to compress the poly-filled bumpers or shocks can cause the bag to deploy at a low speed.

Many people say they were involved in a frontal impact and the bag just fell out. I think the problem here is caused by demonstrations at auto shows and on TV that show the bag deploying like a big pillow that stays inflated for several seconds. The reality is that the bag deploys and deflates in approximately 20 milliseconds, so people who close their eyes during the impact simply miss seeing the air bag inflated. The only other issue I can think of that raises questions is that most people are not aware that when the bag deploys it is common to sustain burns on your arms. The reason is of course that the bag is larger than the steering wheel, so as it inflates, you can get rug rash on your arms.

If the battery cables are cut during a crash will the air bag deploy? Yes, all air bag systems have a standby power unit that is good for about two seconds.

Check Engine Light

Many a trip or vacation has been ruined when the "check engine" light comes on. You can bet it will come on when you are the greatest possible distance from a dealer. What does it mean and what should you do about it? Although it very seldom means there is an actual problem with the engine itself, you should first look at the gauges to be sure the oil light or the engine temperature light are not on. If one or both are on, shut the car off and check the level of the oil or water. If it was the water temperature, leave the hood up for at least 10 minutes before you remove the radiator cap.

In order for an engine to perform within government-regulated exhaust emission levels, the engine management computer has to receive input signals from a lot of components so it can keep the engine at its optimum level of clean emissions. If any of these input signals is missing, the computer will turn on the check engine light to let you know that your engine no longer meets the required emission levels.

Almost all of the computers have a built in "limp home" mode, which means the computer will go to a set of default settings that will allow you to get your car to the dealer. It will not run as well as you would like it to, but as long as there are no other lights on it is safe to drive. When you get to the dealer, give them as much information as possible about the exact driving conditions when the light came on. The check engine light causes frustration for both the customer and the mechanic.

Check engine light incidents account for probably 50% of the letters received by customer relations departments, regardless of make or model of vehicle. Emission standards are very sensitive—the price we must pay to clean our air and leave a better environment for our children. Several manufacturers have widened the parameters to avoid customer letters and to help get better scores on the JD Powers customer satisfaction survey. However, it wasn't legal for them to do this and some face fines that run into the hundreds of millions of dollars. Design engineers are constantly working to improve the reliability of the systems and there is constant pressure on the suppliers to keep the quality of their components at a high level. Try to be a little more understanding the next time your check engine light goes on.

One tip I have for you is to not fill up your gas tank with the engine running and don't keep filling your tank to get an even amount of money once the pump clicks off. Both of these actions can cause the check engine light to go on.

Although it has nothing to do with check engine lights, since I am talking about filling up the gas tank, I should mention that I get a lot of questions about the rotten egg smell from the exhaust. If the check engine light is out, there is likely not a problem with your car. The problem is in the amount of sulphur in the brand of gas you are using. Switch brands and grade of gasoline if you don't want to deal with the smell. The higher grades have less sulphur, so until reformulated gas is standard you will have to live with some smell.

Unintended Acceleration

Because a television news program almost ruined a car company doing a story about the alleged problem of unintended acceleration, I wanted to say a few words about it. Although it seems most people saw that program, few read the two-page ads explaining that the government found that no such condition existed. The story aired sometime around 1985. And since then and 1994, I have had to inspect at least 50 claims a year for this condition. I have had customers leave their car halfway through the back wall of their garage for a week, with the front half in the house, waiting for me to inspect the car. Of course, I never found a problem.

The fact is that even if the engine could go to full acceleration if you have your foot hard on the brakes, the car is not going anywhere. I always examined the brakes but so far have never found a problem. The problem is that people thought they had their foot on the brake but it was in fact on the gas pedal. By 1992, all models of the product that I represent had shift locks installed, which requires that you have the brakes applied before you can engage a gear. I have had no cases on cars newer than 1992, which proves the point.

Service Items

How often should you change your oil? Most car companies say every 5,000 miles if you have a turbo-charged engine and every 10,000 miles on a normally aspirated engine. If you like your car and plan to keep it a long time, 4,000 and 8,000 miles is a much better idea.

What about synthetic oil versus mineral-based oil? I have used synthetic oil since 1977 in my race cars and my family cars. The synthetic base is much better when it comes to staying on the moving parts. This means that if you run low on oil, you stand a better chance of not damaging your engine. It is important to understand, however, that the additives used for anti-foaming, acid, carbon, and so forth, are the same as those used with a mineral-based oil. I don't recommend extending the intervals between oil changes by more than 2,000 to 3,000 miles beyond the normal intervals. I do know of several police departments that switched to synthetic and moved their oil change intervals to 15,000 miles with no problems. But I still wholeheartedly believe that oil changes are cheap insurance, so I would still stand by the 2,000 to 3,000 suggestion. You should hold off on switching to synthetic oil until your engine is broken in, which takes about 5,000 miles. I also recommend using only the manufacturer's oil filter.

The car battery is usually neglected—until the car won't start. It is very important to have your battery serviced every 5,000 or so miles to be sure the terminals are clean and it has the correct level of water. Do not use tap water, which has too much iron and other impurities that sink to the bottom of the batter and will eventually short out the plates. Use only distilled water. In hot climates check the water level every week if you can; it will save you money in the long run.

How many times have you seen cars driving on a cold wet day, with the windows so fogged up the driver is looking through one spot that he or she has to keep wiping? Unless there is a problem with the heater/defroster system, the problem is likely caused by the knob being set on recirculate. It has to be set to pull in outside air, otherwise you are just pulling the moisture up from the carpets and fogging up your windows.

Recently I was asked to look at a car that had paint bubbling on all the vent knobs. It took me a while to realize what happened. The owner of the car had sprayed perfume into the vents to make the car smell nice. The alcohol and various other ingredients in the perfume lifted the paint on the surfaces that were painted. There are sprays made for this purpose, so please don't use perfume!

Fire

Here is a subject I am not very fond of but it happens. When it happens in my territory, I get to try to find out the reason. I have attended at least six courses in fire investigation, but my level of success in determining the exact cause is generally proportionate to the how badly burned the car is. This is also true even for the people who do fire investigations for a living. There are some known problems with some models in every manufacturer's history so the tendency is to blame that part. If the car is old, it is generally fair to assume it was a cracked fuel hose. Unless the fire started inside the car then you assume it was an electrical short, and even though the car is burned to a shell, there are things about the wiring that can tell a story.

Let me tell you a story that involves a fire investigation. The reason I want to share this with you is not because it was a fire, but it is my way of explaining how spending 40 years of your life in the car business effects the way you look at cars. You have to be conscious at all times of the importance of cars to people. In the business we tend to look at cars as very replaceable, so we do not have much if any emotion when we look at a wrecked or burned car, but the owner does.

In this case, the car burned to the ground in the customer's driveway. The customer saw flames inside the car and called the service department at his local dealer. This of course took five or six minutes before the service manager answered the phone. Clearly, the customer should have called the fire department immediately. In any event, I arrived a few days later to see if I could determine what caused the fire. It was at least 90 degrees Fahrenheit that day, but I dutifully put my coveralls on over my shirt and pants and climbed into this burned-out shell with a three-pronged garden tool to dig in the rubble on the floor of the car for evidence. The family had gathered around a picnic table drinking iced tea, watching me. After about a half hour or so, I stuck my head out the window (there was no glass), and said to the owner, "Is it okay if I smoke in your car?" I expected a laugh but got an evil look instead, which brought me back to the reality of the emotion people have for their cars. We all need that kick in the pants sometimes.

That story is my reminder about watching what I say because of people's emotions about their car. This story is about watching your mouth in general. It was a cold day in December many years ago. I was the service manager of a small import dealership in a suburb of Chicago. A car pulled up to the door. Two nuns got out and said they had just had snow tires put on at a tire dealer and the car had a bad vibration. I pointed out that theirs was a front-wheel drive car and the tires were installed on the rear wheels. Because we were busy at the time, rather than ask a mechanic to change the wheels and check the balance, I did it myself. I did not have to balance the wheels because the tire place had not tightened one of the wheels. When I was done one of the nuns asked how much they owed me. Without thinking, I said, "Ah, sh—, that's okay. Just say a prayer for me."

She stared at me and said, "You certainly need it," and left.

Another incident took place at a Chicago-area dealer. A woman and her daughter came in to the service write-up area. They were loudly complaining about the problem they were having with their car. The service writer called me over and explained the problem, which was a crease in the fender the customers felt should be covered by warranty. Well, not only was the car five years old and out of warranty, but the fender crease was caused when the daughter found she was too far forward at the bank drive-through and backed up with the door open. I explained to the mother that this was not a warranty matter. She told me that since I was the factory rep, I could cover it under warranty if I wanted to. I said I would not.

She told me I looked like a nice guy but I was a jerk. I shrugged and said, "That's what my wife says," and walked away. Of course, my wife never said it, but I thought it was an apt rebuttal.

A similar incident happened on the service drive, and again the customer was being very noisy with the service writer, so he called me over to talk to her. The problem in this case was a cracked windshield the woman said should be covered under warranty. Since stress cracks are covered under warranty but windshields hit by stones are not, I took a look. When I lifted the wiper blade to look for the start of a crack it was obvious that it started from a stone chip about half an inch from the molding. Stress cracks always start under the molding. I pointed this out to her and suggested she call her insurance company to get the windshield replaced. After two minutes of ranting and raving, she went away in a huff.

Another time, when I was the distributor service manager for one of the independent distributors, we were having a lot of problems with parts or, rather, the lack of parts. Each month we placed a stock order with the importer and they submitted the order to Japan. Two months in a row, the importer lost the order, which put us in a world of hurt with the dealers and the customers. I think you can imagine what it was like for the customer relations person taking calls from customers whose cars were in various states of disassembly at the dealerships.

It got to the point that the person I had in customer relations refused to take any more calls about parts, so I had to. One of the customers, who used his car as a messenger service, became belligerent and threatening when I told him it might be two weeks before we could complete the repairs to his transmission. I hung up on him.

Several hours later, I looked out my office window and saw a man headed for my office. He was a tall, slender man in his late twenties, and I did not have to be a rocket scientist to realize he was angry. I opened the door to my office and asked him how I could help him. He explained between expletives that he was the man with the transmission problem and if I could not get the parts by the next day to complete the repairs to his transmission, he would blow the place up. He pointed to the door of the warehouse at a boy about eight years old holding a bottle with a rag in it. Perhaps it's because I am from Ireland, but I suffer from severe knee knocks when I see a bomb (no, I never found out if it was gas or water in the bottle). I knew from our earlier conversation what parts he needed for his transmission so I took him back to the training room, dissembled the training transmission, and gave him the parts he needed.

I didn't call the police or even tell my boss. My boss was recovering from bypass surgery and I felt this might have a bad effect on him. And I think I felt sorry for the customer because his car was his livelihood, plus having the police and press involved would have made the company look bad and I already had too much aggravation in my life.

Another incident I found troubling was just a few years ago. I had just finished an inspection of a car that hit a wall across the ally from the customer's garage. The customer, a man in his seventies, asked me what I had found. I told him there was nothing wrong with the car, but the incident had been caused by misapplication of the pedals. He became very upset and said he would accept this explanation for now but if anything like this happens again, he would find where I lived and come after me. In fact he called customer relations the next day and told them the same thing. I suppose none of us likes to be told we made a mistake. Some just take it harder than others!

I said earlier that determining the cause of a fire is proportionate to how badly burned it is, but once in a while you get lucky. Here is what happened to me on a fire investigation many years ago: The information I had was that the car caught fire in the customer's garage during the night. Several months later, I was looking at the car in a junkyard, which was just a shell and surprising to me it was also a diesel engine. I figured the only thing I could do was to take some pictures for my report, which would read "cause could not be determined."

While I was taking the pictures, I was bitten by a bug and my arm swelled up. I walked back to the office of the salvage yard to ask if they had something I could put on my arm. The owner asked me if I had found any reason for the fire. I told him I had no idea, but I was confused by the fact that some bushings under the car were burned that you would not expect to burn. He asked if it could have anything to do with the van? He then led me to a burned out van and said it had been in the fire with the car. The van had been burned to the point that the plastic gas tank was no longer there, so in fact it was the van that burned and when the tank melted the fire went under the car and caught it on fire. But the customer had never said anything about the van. Why? I didn't know, but I was happy to close my report with an explanation of what did happen. Sometimes it's better to be lucky than good.

Two more tips about fires: If you have an older car or a car with lots of miles on it, have the fuel lines and hoses checked for cracks or corrosion. If you have the misfortune to have a fire in your car that starts under the hood, don't panic. It takes at least 10 minutes for the flames to come through from under the hood into the car. Of course the smoke will come through sooner, but if there is something important in the glove box, take the few seconds to get it out. If the fire starts inside the car, get the heck out of there immediately. Although cars do not explode when they burn as you see in the movies (that is done with special effects), the flames will flare when the gas tank catches fire, so stay well away from the car and let the fire department do the rest.

You Tell Me

Regardless of what business you are in I am sure you have situations or explanations of problems that at first make no sense, some that never make sense. Here are a few you can add to your list.

The first little story happened many years ago, so I have had a lot of time to think about it but I still don't understand it. Customer relations asked if I could meet with a customer concerning a steering problem the dealer could not resolve. I was only six hours away, so I drove there that night and was at the dealership at nine the next morning. (Why nine and not eight? Well, no service manager wants to see a factory guy until the morning rush is over.) I met the customer, who told me that when the steering was pointed straight ahead, the spokes of the steering wheel were about 5 or 6 degrees off being completely straight and level. This can be fixed with an alignment and I do not want to get into why the dealer did not fix it. But I asked the customer why it was so critical that it be perfect. Her answer was, "How else can I back out of a parking spot?"

The next situation did not happen to me; it involved one of my counterparts with a domestic manufacturer. A friend sent it to me over the Internet. The story begins with a customer contacting the customer relations department. This gentleman wrote to say that he had a very unusual problem with his car, but he needed to give some background about him and his family to properly explain the situation. He said they were a very close family and liked to maintain certain routines. One of their routines was that after dinner they would vote on what flavor ice cream to have for dessert. When it was decided, Dad would drive to a local grocery store and purchase the ice cream. The problem was that if he bought vanilla ice cream, the car would not start. If he purchased any other flavor the car would start just fine.

The company sent a technical rep to the customer to see if he could witness this situation first-hand. He arrived at the designated time and the customer went into the store and purchased a carton of vanilla ice cream. When he tried to start the car, it would not start. The next evening they repeated the trip but this time the customer bought chocolate ice cream and the car started just fine.

We all know that having ice cream in the car, regardless of the flavor, does not cause a starting problem. The rep asked the customer to go through the steps of purchasing vanilla ice cream and walk back to the car, timing it with a stopwatch. He then asked the customer to go through the process again but this time purchase chocolate ice cream. It took almost five minutes longer to purchase the chocolate ice cream because the vanilla ice cream was in a small freezer at the front of the store and the flavors were all the way in the back of the store. In the short time it took to purchase the vanilla ice cream, the fuel would peculate, so the car would not start. The extra time it took to purchase a flavor ice cream allowed the fuel to cool down a bit and so the car started.

This next story also involved meeting a customer at 7:00 PM , but in this case, it was the only time the customer could get away from work. She had a current year model car and the problem was noise. As we drove and I questioned her more, she said it was not the type of noise that happens over bumps, but it was the difference between when the car was new and now. I still did not understand what she meant. She likened it to a nude painting. She said when the car was new it was as though the cellulite was painted with a feather and now it was painted with a brush. What she meant was that the sound level of the exhaust had changed and she did not like it.

When we got back to the dealership, the district manager, service manager, and I explained that there was no problem with her car and therefore the exhaust would not be replaced. She said that if the exhaust was not replaced, she did not want the car. We pulled the dealer demo alongside her car to prove that they sounded the same. She started the demo put it in gear and took off; in fact, the service manager had to dive onto a snow bank to avoid being hit. The next day the service manager tried calling her at work to tell her if she did not return the car he would have to report it as stolen. The place where she worked told the service manager for several days that she was busy and could not be reached. They finally said she had a nervous breakdown due to work-related stress and was in hospital. I hope she had a complete recovery.

Factories, Importers, and Distributors

The daily routine of factories, importers, and distributors has a trickle-down effect on mechanics. Let's talk first about some of the things that happen in factories.

People often ask me if there is such a thing as a "Monday morning" car. To some extent there is. Once the line starts up after the weekend, those on the line aren't always up to speed as quickly as they should be, so mistakes happen. Of course, if everything else is working as it should, errors are caught during final inspection.

The most often used word in any plant is "quality." This is nothing new, but the word has a different meaning today than it did 10 years ago. Many of us remember when "Made in Japan" referred to toys and trinkets of a very low quality. By the late 1960s, cars from Japan were little more than copies of European cars. I remember shortly after I arrived in America my boss placed an advertisement in the newspaper. It had my picture and a caption that read, "Let an expert handle your foreign car," with a list of the cars on which I was supposed to be an expert. One of the names I had never heard of. I later saw one of these cars and was amazed at how close it was to a well-known British car. The Japanese went on to design and build their own cars, and by the late 1980s they had set the standard for quality.

Because I worked in a Japanese car factory as quality assurance manager and visited some European and American factories around that same time, I can explain some of the differences.

While I was working in a Japanese factory, it was obvious the plant workers were a team; in other factories, workers were just a group. Workers in the Japanese factory held meetings each week to discuss with the team leader ideas on what would lessen the chances of mistakes. The progress of each new idea was followed closely and charted on graphs. At the end of each month a panel, on which I sat, judged the best ideas to be successfully implemented and awards were given. One of these winning suggestions addressed was for a large mirror to be installed on each side of the line so workers could make sure the door sills on each side had the same brand name.

On one occasion I took my staff to an American factory (I am sure it could just as easily have been European) to see firsthand the differences between our factory and a typical American factory. Being from the quality department, we were most interested in the final inspection area. The most glaring difference was that in the Japanese factory if there was a problem with a door fit, the car made a left turn off the line and into the repair shop. It was not an actual shop but a place off the final inspection area where the doors were adjusted by skilled body men. Then the car went to the shipping lane. In the American factory we were visiting, however, as the cars came off final inspection there were workers running along with the car using blocks of wood to try to force the door to fit. At a certain point they let the car go to the shipping lane and began the process all over again on the next car. My staff could hardly believe their eyes.

In the past seven or eight years, most factories I have visited now seem to use a form of the team system and I no longer see anyone running with a car to get the doors to work. I am told that one of the reasons for the door fit being so much better now is when it is installed on the body to go to the paint shop, the adjustments are measured by lasers. When the body comes out of the paint shop, the doors are removed and go to the area where they are built to the specs of the car they will go on. When that car arrives at the area where the doors are installed, robots know the measurements made by the laser and install the door in the exact position as before it went to the paint shop. This process has cut out most of the fit problems with doors.

Quality inspection is a ritual that takes place every day; a random car is picked off the line and inspected by a team of specially trained nitpickers. They write all the faults they find on the car on a large board and assign each fault score depending on how bad the fault is up to a max of 10 (some plants use a 100-point scale) for any one fault. The total allowable faults per car is 12. At some point during the day, all the group managers gather around the board and the factory manager arrives to review the results.

I have witnessed many of these inspections. It is not a pretty sight to see the group leaders fall all over themselves trying to explain when they will correct the process that caused the faults. As I understand it, most factories have always had such a system. It is just that the quality of Japanese cars made them raise the bar. Most of you reading this book will remember the complaints about too many Japanese cars being allowed into the country. The worry was that the non–Japanese manufacturers were worried about not being able to get up to the same level of quality because they had been complacent for so long. Since very little was done to slow down the import of Japanese cars, the competitive battle was on. The result was that the quality of all the manufacturers is at a very high level.

I am sure most of you have heard the term "just-in-time" (JIT). It means that the factory does not have to have a warehouse of parts as in the old days. The suppliers either have a building close to the factory where they warehouse the parts or they actually build the parts in a building close to the factory. They then deliver the parts on schedule to the factory, depending on the production rate of the factory that day. The drawback to this system is that there is no time for inspection of these parts. So how does the factory know the parts are good? The suppliers are chosen well in advance of a new model of car going into production. Prior to actual production there are try-out cars and preproduction cars. Each supplier is required to supply a test batch of parts, each of which is inspected for quality. If one part fails the inspection the entire lot is sent back. This process continues until the supplier can deliver complete lots of parts with no flaws. No further inspections will be done on parts from that supplier unless there is a problem.

Let me give you an example of this process. Four or five months into production we had received quite a few warranty claims for one particular part, even though the supplier had passed the lot inspections. We requested the dealers to send the bad parts back to us for inspection. What we found was that the date codes on the failed parts were from the a period during which this supplier had not passed the lot inspections. The supplier did not destroy the bad parts; they waited until they knew the parts would not be inspected and slipped in some bad parts.

There was a very unpleasant meeting between the top management from the supplier and top management of the factory to iron out the financial ramifications. But the trust factor with the supplier had been damaged and full inspection of all parts was required for the next several shipments, which meant additional manpower. Thankfully, this is the exception rather than the rule, but it underscores how the greed of this supplier hurt the reputation of the factory before anyone realized what had happened.

Not all of the problems that are reported back to the factories are caused by the suppliers, but they are all prioritized and researched by the quality department. Here's an example of the follow-up. In this case, the report was of an under-hood fire. Since that type of report has a high priority, two engineers were dispatched the very next day to the dealership where the problem occurred. What they found was what seemed to be a razor cut in the fuel hose, which sprayed a fine mist of gas onto the exhaust, starting the fire. The fortunate part was that the car was just pulling out of the service department, so a mechanic grabbed a fire extinguisher and put the fire out in a very short time. The engineers started their investigation on the assembly line where the fuel hose was installed and found the person who was installing them caused the problem. When he got a new box of fuel lines, he used a utility knife to cut the box top off and cut several hoses each time. The factory had to alert all the dealers to check every car.

Most American car manufacturers are headquartered in Detroit, with regional locations around the country. Most imports are headquartered on the East Coast. Even with these differences, the functionality of their areas of responsibility are quite similar. There are about 60 administrative departments in most headquarters; the following is a list of the 10 most typical:

- Executive management
- Marketing
- Distribution
- Product management
- Warranty
- Public relations
- Human resources
- Customer and product support
- Legal
- Regulatory compliance

Every time there is a reorganization (the fancy name for "downsizing") the name of the sub groups under these main headings changes.

The interesting thing about working for a manufacturer and calling on dealers is that with the exception of perhaps the dealer him- or herself, most of the employees think we have a glamourous job. I am constantly being asked, "How can I get a job like yours?" I generally tell people the first thing they have to do is send a resume. Nothing can happen if they don't have a resume on file with the human resources department. The next question is, "How did you get started as a factory representative?" Let me tell you how that happened.

I was working in an import car dealership in Florida. The Saturday shift was supposed to alternate between four of us. But it was almost a weekly routine that at about 9:00 AM, I would get a call to come into work because no one else had shown up. On one such Saturday the district service manager from one of the factories came in with a problem with his car. He had several members of his family with him. They were on vacation from England. It was about 10:00 AM and I had at least an hour more work to complete on the car in my stall. I ended up working well beyond my noon shift end until about 4:00 that afternoon, fixing his car. He was so happy to have his car for the weekend that he invited me for dinner that night.

He told me that the company was going to make him the competition manager and if I was interested he would recommend me as his replacement. In borrowed clothing, I interviewed for the position. I got the job, and as they say, the rest is history! It was really just a matter of being in the right place at the right time.

An interesting note about having been a factory representative is that assuming you did a good job, getting a position with another factory that has an opening is not difficult. It is a network somewhat like a big circle and it is difficult for an outsider to get in.

Let's look at some of the processes in these headquarters that trickle down to the dealer level. Change at the top executive level, and their use of consulting firms, has serious ramifications for employees. They usually have to reapply for their positions, titles and territories are changed, and so forth. It often takes a year for the employees and dealers to figure out who is responsible for what. I have been through four reorganizations and two things have changed: Total staff has been reduced by several hundred people and we now work from offices in our homes (which unfortunately are not tax deductible) without the risk of an audit. The amount of work per person has been increased (my 10-hour day had become a 12-hour day) since there are no longer secretaries to do your typing and you simply can't get away from your office anymore. I find it more difficult to work at home as the rest of my family expect me to run errands and so forth, since I am at home. As a close friend of mine who runs a consulting company told me, "If you get into consulting never get involved in the implementation only in the recommendations." I can hardly stand a job with this much glamour.

Marketing and advertising are other areas that effect every one down the line. I know the advertising people use focus groups to review the advertisements before they use them, but some of the ads are downright embarrassing and are not likely to sell cars. During a recent visit to one of my dealers, I was discussing this subject with the dealer principal. A wonderful person—of course he is; he came up through the back end as a mechanic and service manager before he became a dealer principal—he showed me a series of ads that are used in Europe for our product. They were fabulous compared to the ads that are made in the United States. I have no idea why we don't use them.

Of course the marketing people do not make these ads; they use very expensive advertising companies to come up with the ideas. The things the marketing people are directly responsible for pertain to the content of the car itself such as color, equipment, accessories, and so on. If you consider how far ahead they have to make their decisions, I think they do a great job.

There are two areas in which the marketing people demanded something from the factory and got it, but this has lead to customer complaints.

I previously mentioned low-profile tires. I said that if you live in a very mild climate with smooth roads they are great; unfortunately, most of the country's climate is not mild. And there are potholes to contend with. So the amount of money spent on blown tires and bent wheels on cars with 40 or 45 profile tires is high, which does not make customers happy.

The other issue is radio reception—or the lack thereof. This is an issue many customers have raised with me. Years ago I was traveling with a radio engineer; he was doing a survey of my dealers to get their opinion of the radio in our cars, which his company supplied. I asked him why during the 1960s and 1970s, I could listen to a baseball game for at least 400 miles, now even a 50,000-watt station faded out at 200 miles or less. He explained that the marketing people were demanding more features for cars but space for the radio has not increased. Receivers are much smaller today. In addition, years ago, there was a tuning knob and an external antenna. Now most antennas are in the windshield or rear window, which protects them against vandals and carwashes, but doesn't give the best reception.

The human resources department comes to mind as another area that impacts everyone. When I was interviewed by a headhunter to work for a manufacturer as a quality assurance manager, the salary I was quoted before the interview was different than what I was actually offered. The salary was $8,000 short of what the headhunter told me. I spoke to the head of human resources, who told me their lower offer was top of the scale of the position I'd applied for. This was on a Tuesday and I was supposed to fly to Japan on Saturday. Well, I knew I was their only candidate, so I played hardball and was able to get the higher salary. Later I found out several of my peers were making quite a bit more than me.

When I was hospitalized because of a flutter in my heart caused by stress on the job, my wife Cindy and I discussed the possibility of my seeking another job. The decision was made for me on the third day of my hospital stay when I was awakened by a priest who he said he wanted to anoint me. He explained that you don't have to be dying to receive last rites, but it still scared the you-know-what out of me. I decided I was not going to allow a job to do this to my health.

I talked to one of the Japanese importers in California I had been told needed an experienced technical rep. The phone conversation was very positive, so an interview was arranged for the following Monday. The gentleman I talked to assured me that the salary would be a certain dollar amount and that this figure had been approved by top management. I flew out on Sunday night and went through the formal interview, including a physical, Monday morning. Everything was a go until I met with human resources. They didn't want to pay me the salary I'd requested, so I left.

My most recent experience with salaries is that when the company I currently work for hired me, I did not get raises for several years because they said they had hired me at the top of the range. I liked the job and the product well enough that it made it easy to accept what they were saying even if I did not necessarily believe it.

Following the last reorganization with my present company, which took place one and a half years ago and is the fourth reorganization in 10 years, top management decided to hire more technical people in the field. The idea behind that was to give the dealers better technical support.

It sounded like a great idea except they set it up in what they call "market areas" based on sales volume. I truly don't understand the way they set up the areas (which brings me back to my friend's statement about consulting companies—make the recommendations and get out). Now I cover 30 dealers in a nine-state area; and some of my peers have only two dealers to handle, some have six or seven. In the larger dealerships, there is at least one shop foreman helping the mechanics, plus the mechanics share information or bounce problems off each other. So they don't need to call the technical rep as often as the small dealer with one or two mechanics.

The next inexplicable human resources decision has to do with salaries. As will happen in every company, people talk and it did not take long to find out that the new people being hired, none of whom had any experience, were being paid as much or more than those of us who had been on the job a decade or more. In this case, one of the new guys had been recommended by one of our seasoned veterans and so when he received a written offer, he showed it to the veteran. Imagine how the veteran felt when he saw that the offer was more than he was making after 12 years. He went to his direct boss to ask what he was going to do about it. His boss recommended that if he didn't like it, he should quit. That attitude didn't do much for morale. But then, these are the same people who come up with bonus criteria you need a lawyer to interpret. Forms for your individual planning session (ISP) take several hours to fill out, then your boss ignores them and comes with his own version, which you have no choice but to sign. I know a lot of human resources people personally and they are great people, but when they put on their corporate hats they make some strange decisions.

The warranty department probably has the most impact on the mechanics. One of the primary functions of a warranty department is number crunching; there is probably no statistic they don't track. They run weekly reports of the top 20 claims by cost and item to alert the factory of any sudden increase in the failure rate of any part. They also run trend analyses of all dealers using groups of similar size, units in operation, and sales volume. If a dealer is out of line with some type of repair, the district manager will be alerted. It then becomes the district manager's job to visit the dealer to find the reason for the out-of-line condition. The district manager will do a mini-audit of about a hundred repair orders. If a bad trend is discovered, the district manager will request the audit team from headquarters come in and do a full audit—not something a dealer wants, believe me.

Even without the audits, dealers look upon the warranty department much like a gestapo outfit because of their rules, which many dealers believe are made simply to avoid paying claims. Having been on both sides of this issue, I believe most of these rules are checks and balances put in place because the claims are electronically submitted. A person does not review them unless an out-of-line trend shows up in the statistical analyses. The warranty department has to plug up as many loopholes as possible. Do the dealers look for loopholes? Of course they do. But in general they are not trying to cheat; they are trying to find ways to get claims through without an authorization.

For example, say a customer comes in with a car at 6,000 miles complaining that the windshield wipers do not clean the windshield very well. Windshield wipers are a "wear" item (such as wipers, brake pads, and clutch) and these are not covered under warranty. They are warranted for a defect not wear. But the service manager agrees with the customer that they should last longer than 6,000 miles, so he installs a new set on the car and sends the customer on his way.

The correct procedure for the service manager to follow is to hold the claim until an authorization from the district manager to submit the claim is received. The problem is that because factory people in general have to attend so many meetings, it can be up to a month before he or she comes in to write authorizations. In the meantime the service manager has to pay the mechanics, so all the claims he is sitting on for authorizations become receivable. Since no business wants to sit on receivables, in this type of situation, the warranty clerk will put the claim through as a broken wiper so it goes through without an authorization. Very large dealers are self-authorizing up to a certain dollar amount so they don't have to sit on so many claims.

Now let's look at some of the things warranty departments do that raise the mechanics blood pressure. I could fill an entire book with warranty stories, but I will limit it to just a few.

On the end of each drive axle—that's the shaft that goes from the transmission to the wheels to drive the wheels (front wheel drive)—is a joint to allow the axle to move up and down with the suspension. Each of these joints has a rubber boot over them to retain grease. We had a problem with these boots cracking and losing the grease so we were replacing a lot of them under warranty. The flat rate book allowed 48 minutes to replace the boot. The mechanics were happy to do the job because like any job you do a lot, you get to be fast at it and that is how they make money.

Eventually, the factory changed the material of the boot and issued a recall to change all the boots. Now here is the kicker: They changed the flat rate time to 0.8 hours for both sides, or 24 minutes per side. The people in the warranty department were trying to save the company money. The reality was that the mechanics could not do the repair in 40 minutes, so most of them would only replace the boot that was leaking at the time and charge for both. Dishonest? Sure. But I would have done the same thing. When the factory realized what was going on, they sent out a new bulletin, increasing the time allowance, but the claim had to be accompanied by both old boots in order for it to be paid.

Recently, a mechanic pointed out to me that we (the company I work for) reduced the flat rate time by 0.2 twice on one operation to the point where he can no longer beat the time.

Another recent situation is a bulletin from the warranty department about a particular check engine light code for which claims will be paid once only. We were receiving two or three claims on the cars that had this code. The problem the mechanics were having was that they could not make the problem repeat when the car came into the shop. So they would spend several hours checking the system, tightening clamps, and so on without finding any particular problem. They would drive the car as much as 100 miles and have no problem. Two weeks later the car would be back with the same code. I assure you, the mechanic wants that car back even less than the customer or the factory. What should the mechanic do? What happens is the service manager calls the district manager and the technical specialist and gets the go-ahead to replace all the parts on the system. If the service manager is not familiar with the bulletin or does not get the factory guys involved, the claim will not be paid.

I have worked for four different factories and warranty people are good people just doing their job. I know the pressure they are under to reduce warranty costs, but I wish they would consider the effect the decisions they make have on the mechanics. It seems that every time a decision is made to reduce the time allowance or change the rules of what they will pay, a few more mechanics get out of the business.

Since we are talking about flat rate I have to tell you a story about my ego and flat rate. I was visiting a dealer in Detroit many years ago, the company I was working for had just come out with a new model.

The dealer said his demo needed a clutch and his mechanic said the flat rate was just 3.5 hours—impossible. I disagreed and said the repair could be done in an hour and a half. The dealer said he had a $20 bill that said I could not replace the clutch on that car in less than 3.5 hours. I put on my coveralls and went to work. Less than two hours later, the car had a new clutch installed. The dealer handed me the $20 and thanked me for the cheapest clutch job he ever had. I assure you I have not allowed my ego to do that to me again.

Customer Relations

I don't care what industry you are talking about—cars, boats, computers—they all have a customer relations department. The idea of talking to unhappy customers all day does not appeal to me, so I commend these people. As with all departments in the auto industry, the way they function changes with each reorganization. At one point in time they had the power to make on-the-spot decisions for the customer and in fact override the decision of the district manager. I am told this is no longer the case; they now take the information from the customer and pass it on to the proper person for follow-up. They then monitor the progress of the case and keep the customer informed until the case is closed.

The major complaint most of us have about calling any customer relations department is that it seems to be impossible to talk to a live person. It seems that you always end up leaving a message or sending a letter, but I guess that is the world we live in. No doubt some manager was praised for installing this system and reducing staff.

Is it any different with independent distributors? I have worked for two; the first was owned by a man who was a disgrace to the car business. His god was money and what he had to do or how he had to treat people in his pursuit of becoming rich meant nothing to him. This man wrote the book when it came to harassing secretaries into performing sex acts, but they did not have the nerve or the money to sue him. As far as the car business is concerned, we would go as long as six months with no training instructor because no one would work for what he paid. So the mechanics in our area were not very well trained and the cars were not fixed properly, which caused me to go through customer relations people like money at an amusement park. The factory finally bought him out for millions and have done a good job over the past eight years or so of regaining the product's reputation.

The second independent distributor I worked for was the exact opposite; it is still in business run by the same two gentlemen. They are good to the employees and do a great job with the product.

What Has Changed the Job of Being a Mechanic?

At the start of the book, I mentioned how cars have changed over the years and how different and difficult the job of a mechanic has become as a result. But as I take you down that road of change, I will also try to explain how some of these changes have made our lives better and safer.

Emission controls began the use of computers to monitor the systems on a car. It all started in California in the 1960s when the farmers discovered brown spots on their lettuce. Scientists determined they were caused by pollution (smog). I will not get into what it takes to make smog but hydrocarbons (HC) are a main contributor. Because the smog caused severe economic problems for the crop growers the California Air Resource Board (CARB) began legislation to reduce emissions from cars and industrial plants. By the early 1970s most manufacturers had at least an exhaust gas recirculation (EGR) system on the engine, which a lot of us remember caused a rough idle and a lack of power.

Here is a true story that happened in 1973. I was the service manager at a dealership west of Chicago. One of my good customers was a name familiar to and loved by all: Mr. Paul Harvey, a man who is just as nice in person as he sounds on the radio. His son, Paul Junior, needed a new car so he came to the dealership to test drive the new models. When he came back from the test drive he asked about the car's idle and lack of power compared to his old car. I explained to him that it was the combination of EGR and the lean mixture required to meet the emissions and there was nothing that could be done to change it. He decided to put off buying a car for a few years until the manufacturers had more time to work out the bugs.

They did, of course, primarily because of the use of computers to control the fuel mixture. I won't get too technical, but when you hear anyone talk about mixture, they are referring to the amount of air and fuel being supplied to the engine. The ideal ratio is 14.7 parts air to 1 part fuel. Of course, that was just the start of the necessary process to clean up the air we breathe. I remember hearing the top executive of a car company say during the 1970s, "They expect us to put cleaner air out the exhaust than we take in the intake."

I have a story to tell; it's unpleasant but does make a point. Several months ago a friend of a mechanic I know decided to take his own life. He ran the car engine with a hose from the exhaust into the car. When they found him, however, he had in fact hanged himself. They figure he realized that with the amount of carbon monoxide from today's cars, it would have taken a long time to kill himself. I am not a chemist, so I will not speculate as to whether that is a fact or not.

Since the early 1970s, all progressions and developments regarding emissions are monitored by the Environmental Protection Agency (EPA) on the national level and California Air Resources Board (CARB) in California, although several East Coast states are adopting the more stringent CARB emission standards. Engine design engineers have done a great deal of work with the basic engine to make it burn cleaner since that time. Before the 1970s, combustion efficiency was poor so a great deal of unused gases went out the exhaust. Even as the engine design changed and became more efficient and cleaner burning, the amount of nitrogen oxides (NOx), hydrocarbons (HC), and carbon monoxide (CO) was too high.

Around 1975, the catalytic converter was used to render these gases harmless to our air. This was a two-stage convertor. Since 1978 the three-stage convertor was developed and an oxygen sensor added. The purpose of the oxygen sensor is to measure the amount of free oxygen ions in the exhaust and feed this information back to the computer so it can determine the richness or leanness of the fuel/air mixture.

Here's a tip on how to remember the four-stroke cycles of a four-stroke engine, which is the basic principal of how the engine in your car works. The four cycles are induction, compression, power, and exhaust. If you can't remember that, then try what I told two women working for me who took a basic engine class and couldn't recall these basics: suck, squeeze, bang, and blow. (I bet they never forgot!)

Also during the past couple decades, the complete engine management system has become computerized. On-board diagnostics (OBD) is now used to indicate that a fault has occurred in the system, with built-in codes to help the mechanic find the problem. By the late 1980s, if a fault occurred, it would also turn on a light on the dash to let the driver know. At that time I could remember all 25 or so fault codes in the engine management system; now there are at least 150. I was just reading an internal publication that said in 1982 the programmed capacity in the management system if written on 8.5-by-11 sheets of paper would have been about an inch thick. Today's management system on the same paper would be 2 feet tall!

By 1994 all manufacturers had to have OBD on the car to monitor the following functional items in the emission system:

- Efficiency of the catalytic converter
- Oxygen sensor or sensors
- Misfiring in the cylinders
- Evaporative control system (EVAP) (for holes in hoses, loose clamps, leaks in valves, the gas tank, or loose or missing gas cap)
- Secondary air system (to add air during warm up and lean out the fuel mixture)
- Fuel system
- Exhaust gas recirculation (EGR) system

The transmission control unit (computer) feeds information to the fuel system computer so that becomes part of the equation. For those of you not in the car business, that is most likely more than you ever cared to know about the fuel system, so let's take a look at some of the other systems that are monitored:

- ABS
- SRS
- Climate control
- Seats
- Instrument cluster
- Alarm

Now here is where it gets tough on the mechanics who are not computer literate. Over the past five years or so, all the monitoring of these systems could be done with a hand-held scanner or you could hook up the scan tool through a computer. What is the difference? Well, if you go through the computer it gives you access to fault tracing steps, bulletins, and so forth, and the scan tool is used in conjunction with the service manuals, bulletin binders tech notes, and so forth. Mechanics who are not comfortable with computers choose the scan tool but soon there will be no more service manuals or bulletins—the information will only be on CD. By the year 2000, I doubt there will be CDs and all of the diagnostic computers will be online with the manufacturer's mainframe.

The main reason there will no longer be service manuals—and I hope you don't consider these next few lines a waste a paper—is, in fact, paper. Consider this: Five years ago the SRS system had one or two sensors and, depending on the manufacturer, about five or six fault codes. The service manual was about 50 or 60 pages. New European cars in 1999 have at least 14 sensors and more than a hundred fault codes. (I trust the same is true of American and Japanese cars as well.) If you assume all systems on the car evolve at the same rate as the SRS system, imagine how thick the service manuals would be. Clearly, this shows the difference between mechanics of the 1960s and 1970s and those of today.

When I discuss this with mechanics who are over 40, their reaction is that they want to get out of this business. They say they can't keep up with all this computer technology; they grew up as I did with carburetors that you could adjust to get the most performance from an engine. With these new cars, the customer will have a choice of horsepower. When the salesman sells the car he will write on the buyers order what horsepower the customer requested. Then when the mechanic performs the predelivery inspection on the car, he can go online with the factory through the computer and download the requested horsepower into the car's main fuel system computer. This is a far cry from adjusting a carburetor!

The switch to multiplexing is simply a case of space and wire, with fewer connectors to go bad.. As more and more power accessories are added to cars, the more wires are added. If you look at the amount of wires going into the door of your car, particularly if you own a luxury car, you will see there are at least 40 wires.

With multiplexing, the amount of wires can be reduced to about seven, so the advantage is obvious. What about the disadvantages? For mechanics, there are a few. First, diagnosis can only be done with a computer so that will make life difficult for the mechanics who don't get along well with computers. Second, you cannot "try" a part from another car because the master, or main, computer will know the part you installed is not one of the "family" and the car will not work. Since it is common practice for all of us in the business to swap parts for the sake of expedience in determining if that part is causing the problem, this will be difficult for all of us.

The point is that most of us got into this business because we love to fiddle with stuff to make it work better. The cars of the future can only be fiddled with if you are an electronics expert.

Surveys

When researching for this book, I spoke with so many mechanics about how they feel about their jobs, their bosses, and so forth, I wondered if they would say the same things on a survey. I tend to be more honest on a survey, so I decided to conduct my own survey so I would get their true feelings in writing. Would their answers be different from what they told me in person?

I felt it would be easier to interpret the results if I did not know who wrote the answers, so I kept them anonymous. Although this is not a scientific survey, it represents mechanics, service managers, and parts managers in seven states. I don't think my results would be any different had I surveyed auto people on the East or West Coast; I have spoken to my peers in those areas and they report the same basic attitudes.

Although I call only on import dealers, a high percentage of them have domestic cars as well. I also faxed some of the surveys to friends of mine who are service managers for domestic dealers, and they had their mechanics fill them out and fax them back to me. I am satisfied that the results are a fair representation of an overall attitude.

Mechanics Survey

How long have you been a mechanic?

The average length of time as a mechanic of those surveyed was 22 years, with the least length of service 8 years and the longest 46. They are mechanics who have been in the business long enough to form a good basis for the survey. In other words they have been around long enough to have a valuable opinion but not so long as to have a cynical attitude, which may be based on something more than the real current condition of being a mechanic.

Do you work on imports or domestic cars?

More than half the mechanics surveyed work only on import cars; however, in the smaller dealerships where both imports and domestic cars are sold, they work on both. I found it interesting that in these shops, the designated and trained import mechanics work on both, but the domestic mechanics don't like to work on the imports. It is also interesting that in a lot of cases I left the survey with the domestic mechanics and most of them did not return them.

Do you think you are fairly treated by the dealership as a person?

I was pleasantly surprised to find that more than half of the mechanics feel that the dealer principals or general managers treat them fairly. There were only six who said "no" and the rest said "most of the time" or "sometimes." I feel that the cornerstone to hiring and keeping good mechanics in the future will have a lot to do with the reputation of the dealer in treating the mechanics financially and as people.

Do you think you are treated fairly by the factory?

By the time I waded through the answers to this question, I thought I must be a very brave person to call on these mechanics every day. With the exception of two of the newer or younger mechanics who said "somewhat," and five from mechanics who work on a particular brand of car that is very generous with flat rate times and diagnosis time, the responses varied from language I don't want to print here to "they screw us," "flat rate times suck," or "could they diagnose the problems in the time they allow us to do it." I'm sure most of the mechanics used the survey to sound off because they believe it will not change.

There are exceptions to every rule, however. Recently I was conducting a lunchtime meeting in a dealership. I was explaining how to fault trace one of the systems on our product that had been causing problems. One of the mechanics became very angry because he felt that the time allowance to go through the procedure was too low. We exchanged some heated words and he left the room. The other 10 mechanics were just happy we now had a procedure that worked.

What is the best thing about being a mechanic?

Most of these answers revolved around the fact that it is a skill that allows you to not only make money in a dealership, but you can also make money on "shade tree work." Shade tree work refers to working on cars at your home for friends, relatives, or a customer base you have built up over the years. This customer base is generally made up of people who can't afford to take their car to the dealer or can't get there during regular hours. The term "shade tree" refers to the fact that most of the mechanics years ago did not have a garage at their homes to work in so, on a hot day they did as much of the work as they could under a big tree. The tree was also used to sling a rope or chain over to pull out an engine.

I too did this type of work when I was a mechanic, though most of the work I did was on race cars. I had a few other regular customers as well. They were two elderly brothers who owned a drug store and usually could not get their car in to a dealer during the work week. One day they had a broken part, so they had no choice but to bring it in and I was the mechanic assigned to the car. When the repair was made, I test drove the car with one of the brothers and he explained their situation to me and asked me if I would be able to do future work on their car. I did this for several years, until their house burned down and they both perished.

I met my other regular customer when I pulled in too tight to let a car go by and ripped the bumper off a parked car. I went to the house and told the owner what had happened, but that I was a mechanic and would take care of it. I did and he became a good customer.

Do dealers get upset with the mechanics if they find out they are doing "shade tree work?" In general, they do not because they know that these are older cars that would not come to them anyway. So as long as the mechanic is not wearing himself out to the point that he can't do his work during the day they don't mind. It also helps the dealers parts business because in general these mechanics buy the parts from the dealership rather than from a supplier because they have a comfort level with using factory parts.

Overall, the majority of the answers to this question talked about the satisfaction they got when a car came in with a problem and left their stall working well.

What is the worst thing about being a mechanic?

The three answers sharing equal billing were: (1) lack of respect, (2) warranty work and how badly it pays for diagnosis time, and (3) technology is moving so fast it is almost impossible to keep up with the changes in the cars and night classes to learn computer skills are necessary. The few answers that did not mention these three issues talked about the stress involved in the job.

If you could change your profession, would you?

The answer to this question was an overwhelming "yes," with the only exceptions being mechanics who had been in the business less than 10 years. This makes sense as they are younger and not intimidated by the shift in technology.

Would you allow your child to become a mechanic?

The answer to this question runs almost parallel with the answers to the previous question. The mechanics who had been in the business fewer than 10 years said "yes" or "most likely." The older mechanics' answers ranged from "no way" to "I would cut his hands off first." I think they are being shortsighted to the extent that there will be a lot of change in the future that will make it a good business to be in. I'll discuss this later in the book.

Do you work flat rate or other?

Flat rate was the only answer to this question, which is an issue I will also talk about later in the book.

How are the benefits at this dealership?

Although four or five said they had no benefits or retirement plan, most had good benefits and those who were also union members looked forward to a decent retirement. Most said they may have to work on a car at home once in a while for extra spending money, but feel they will be okay financially and look forward to retirement.

The Functions of a Service Manager

Most service managers will tell you no matter what goes wrong in the dealership, it always lands on their desk. Having been there, I agree. But what are the actual responsibilities listed on the job description?

Service managers are responsible for hiring service writers, mechanics, warranty clerks, customer follow-up people, porters, and car washers. Once they are hired, the service manager has to establish what training is needed, teach them company policies, and get uniforms. Then, of course, there is always the paper work.

The service manager must establish proper procedures for processing the following:

- Repair orders
- Work distribution

- Time control
- Invoicing
- Customer follow-up
- Filing of all department records and purchases

One of the problems all service managers have is that they can't seem to get out of their offices. They are constantly on the phone with the manufacturer's warranty department, technical hotline, district service manager, or customers. When they get out into the shop, every employee seems to want to talk. Mechanics want the service manager to accompany them on a test drive to find a noise or squeak. In so many cases, the service manager uses test drives to go by the body shop to check on sublet work. The service manager becomes peacemaker, advisor, slave driver, arbitrator, good guy, bad guy—and everything in between.

One of the constant battles for every service manager is keeping up with special tools and equipment. It seems like every hour one of the mechanics can't find a special tool so things get hectic while he tries to find out who used it last. Then there is the lift or some other piece of equipment he has to get a repair person in to fix. By the end of the day he is worn out but not finished as there are the daily time and payroll records to be submitted to the office manager. After that, there may be a meeting to attend.

The biggest nightmares for a service manager are the cars that are not fixed right the first time. The most important things he can do to avoid this are make sure the mechanics have all the training they need. He can also make sure the special tools and equipment are in good working condition and the shop is clean with adequate lighting. Then there is the most important tool of all: communication.

It is important to have regular shop meetings at least once a month after hours where pizza and soda or coffee (never beer) are served. Generally, the meetings should be divided into two segments: The first part should be used to bring the mechanics and service writers up-to-date on any factory or company policies that may have changed. Any service bulletins that have been issued since the last meeting should also be discussed.

The second part of the meeting should give employees the chance to talk about their problems. The service manager should answer what he can and make notes of the questions he can't answer (making sure to respond with the answer as soon as possible). Of course the service manager is ultimately responsible for profitability and customer satisfaction, both of which generate a lot of meetings with the general manager or dealer principal, or both, and the factory rep. (A roll of antacid tablets and some headache pills should be a part of any service manager's office.)

Service Manager Survey

How long have you been a service manager?

The average length of time as a service manager by those who filled out the survey was 20 years, so there is a lot of experience behind these answers. All worked for more than one dealer either as a mechanic or as a service manager

Were you ever a mechanic?

Although being a mechanic is not a prerequisite for being a service manager, all of the service managers who filled out the survey had spent at least two years as a mechanic. One had spent 15 years "twisting wrenches," as we say in the business, which I feel adds to the value of their answers. It is a lot more common to find service managers who spent only a short time as a mechanic and then made the switch. Most long-term mechanics hate paperwork, so they do not want to be a service manager.

Do you feel the dealer treats you with respect?

Almost all of the service managers answered affirmatively, but added comments such as "not as much as he should based on the fact that I am his cash cow."

One of the differences between the service managers and mechanics surveys was the additional comments of the service managers. Some almost wrote a book for me, but overall, they feel the dealer principal is satisfied with the way things are going until the next 20-group meeting. What is that, you ask? Most if not all the manufacturers encourage the dealers to form groups of like size dealers who meet at least twice a year. During these meetings they share their financial statements to review each other's expense and personnel structures to discover how they can help each other to be more profitable. The results of these meetings usually mean that when the dealer principal arrives back at his own dealership, changes will be made. All of the changes will involve cutting expenses, which means more stress for all of the managers.

Do you feel your mechanics are respected by the dealer/GM?

One service manager answered "somewhat," but the rest said "no," which is interesting in that the mechanics generally believe the dealer respects them but the service managers don't. Of course, the service manager deals with the dealer/general manager on a much more personal basis, so he is more aware of comments or statements made by the dealer or general manager than the mechanics.

Does your dealer share reward money received from the factory for high CSI scores?

In many cases this question was left blank, either because the manufacturer does not have a program that involves cash reward or the service manager never earned it. Of those who are a part of such a program most said "yes, under duress," or "yes, a very small portion."

Do you feel the policies of the factory are fair?

I suspected the response to this questions would be a resounding "no," but I felt that I had to ask it. One service manager said the factories were becoming more like the gestapo every day. All the respondents said that in this day and age of so many electronic controls and "check engine" lights relating to emission control problems the factories were too nitpicking. Claims were frequently rejected by the factory for repeat repairs on intermittent problems, which are very difficult to find. The service department feels it is simply trying to satisfy the customer by making an educated guess on which part to replace, based on the customer's complaint, although they often cannot duplicate the problem. There is a lot of hostility about this type of situation.

How difficult is it to find a good mechanic?

All were in agreement that it is becoming very difficult to find a good mechanic. They will try to steal from the competition or offer rewards to their current staff to talk their friends into coming to work at their shop. They all agree that newspaper ads bring almost no responses or only bring in people they would not hire.

Do you use an apprenticeship program?

At this time none of the service managers uses an apprenticeship program. Some said they had in the past. (More about this later.)

Do the local trade schools or community colleges contact you to place graduates?

The answer to this question varied widely, so I am not sure what the true situation is.

Is there a mentor program available through the dealer association?

Just a few service managers said there was a mentor program available through the dealer association. I suspect they are just not aware of it. (I will follow up on this in the next chapter.)

Do you use it?

Even the service managers who were aware of a mentor program do not use it.

If the answer to previous question is "no," would you use a mentor program if available?

When I talked to most of the service managers in person, they indicated they would not use a mentor program. On the survey, however, they said they would. Perhaps they had time to think about it before they filled out the survey. I hope so as I think it's a great idea.

Do you receive good benefits with your dealer?

Most said that they had benefits, although some had none. Many depended on the benefit package from their wives' jobs for insurance.

Would you change your profession if you could?

There were a few positive answers to this question, but many felt they were too old to change.

Parts Department

Does the parts department have a trickle-down effect on the mechanics? You bet it does. Do you remember when I talked about productivity? The number one cause of lost productivity for a mechanic is the time wasted waiting at the parts counter. Recently, I was visiting a fairly large dealer that has a total of 18 mechanics, and I counted 10 of them at one time standing around at the parts counter. Why does this happen? For the most part (no pun intended), it is bad management on behalf of the parts manager and the service manager.

In a well-run dealership there are systems in place so this waiting around doesn't occur. Rather, the parts are waiting for the mechanic by the time he approaches the counter. Thirty years ago I worked in a dealership where I had an intercom on the wall of my stall. I would call the parts department, tell them what

I needed, and they would send a parts runner to me with the parts.

In about 40% of dealerships today, mechanics receive their jobs via a computer terminal in their stall. These terminals are linked to a terminal in the parts department. When a mechanic determines the parts he needs, he types it into the computer, it shows up on the parts terminal, and they have the part pulled by the time he walks over to the parts department.

One of the other things a good parts department will do is to have parts prepackaged for major inspections or tune-ups. This way the mechanic does not have to wait while the parts person picks each part; he is simply handed a package of parts and off he goes.

If the parts department does not have the part the mechanic wants, it is usually not their fault. Inventory levels are controlled by the dollar amount the dealer principal will allow and the usage rate of a part as determined by a computer.

Some small dealers still use a card system, but if a part has never been in stock there will be no usage rate. Mechanics have trouble understanding this concept. If the part is not available, they have to clock off that job, push the car outside, and get another job. There is a lot of time loss, but it is not the parts department's fault. Even so, most of the parts departments run a 95%-plus fill rate, which is acceptable. If your fill rate is too high it means you are stocking way too many old or slow-moving parts, which is not where you want your inventory dollars to be tied up.

Most of the very profitable parts departments have a large wholesale business, which means they have large accounts with body shops and independent repair shops. Between the maintenance of the wholesale accounts watching over the people working the counters (wholesale and retail), the parts department is a great profit center for the dealer.

The parts department is vital to the profitability of the dealership. Do they get the respect they deserve?

Parts Manager Survey

How long have you been a parts manager?

The average response was 15 years.

Do you feel you are treated with respect by the dealer/general manager?

With the exception of the three or four who answered "sometimes" or "most of the time," the parts managers answered affirmatively.

Does the factory give you the help you need to do a good job ?

With the exception of two parts managers who answered simply "no," most wrote small books about the fact that almost all of the factories have the same person calling on the dealership representing parts and service. In most cases, they spent very little time visiting the parts department. When they did, issues that were raised were not followed up on.

What is the best thing about being a parts manager?

The most common answer was "keeping it all together and making a good profit for the dealer."

What is the worst thing about being a parts manager ?

This answer was almost equally divided between "when the shit hits the fan" and "baby-sitting the counter people."

If you could change your profession, would you?

The "yes" and "no" answers were just about equal, with a slight edge toward "no."

If you worked for the factory, what would you change?

Most talked about the frequency of being able to submit stock orders. Some wanted daily stock orders; some two per week. When I was involved in parts, stock orders occurred once a month and I don't feel qualified to comment on the merits of daily stock orders. There are basically three types of orders to the factory: stock orders, supplemental orders, and emergency orders. Stock orders carry the largest discount and free shipping; supplemental orders have a smaller discount and there may be a shipping charge; emergency orders have almost no discount and the dealer pays for the shipping. The goal of the parts manager is to order everything on stock orders.

If you were the dealer principal what would you change ?

These answers were very individualized. Each parts manager took this question to a personal level rather than an overall idea of how the perfect dealer principal or general manager should be involved in the daily running of a parts department. Some type of profit sharing plan was the only thing that was mentioned more than a few times.

What kind of benefits do you receive?

The answers to this question ranged from fair to average; it did not seem to be a big bone of contention.

How is the pay?

I wasn't surprised at the high percentage of "good" or "average" responses because parts managers seem to be a stable group. They like what they do and in most cases have been doing it for a long time. They know the policies and procedures, which gives them a certain comfort level.

Service Writers

One of the most difficult jobs in a dealership is that of service writer. When anyone's car breaks down, the service writer gets the call. The calls range from a polite conversation to a lot of cussing about the product. It takes a special person to deal with the angry calls. When the service manager interviews candidates for this position, he has to be careful not to hire a person with a short fuse. Every car company has training programs in telephone and people skills for service writers, but if the people don't have the proper disposition to start with the training will not help.

Other than dealing with customers who are upset because their car is broken down, explaining to a customer that the repair needed is not covered by the warranty is the most difficult aspect of the service writer's job.

Customers usually only see the service writer twice, once when the repair order is written up and again in the evening when the car is picked up. Between these times, service writers are busy following up on the progress of your car, as well as about 15 others. Additionally, they spend their time answering the telephone, making appointments, and calling wreckers to pick up cars that are broken down.

The service writer is primarily concerned about two things: whether or not the car will be finished on time and whether the mechanic found any other problems.

If the car is not finished when it was promised, the service writer must make arrangements for a loaner or rental car. If the mechanic finds another problem, the service writer must work up an estimate of the cost and call the customer to see if he or she would like the repair made. If the repairs are covered by the new car warranty, the service writer must call the customer to advise that additional repairs are being made. If the repair is covered by warranty, why do they have to call the customer? The reason for this is if a warranty repair was done without a complaint written on the repair order, the factory rep will debit the claim as an add-on repair. All add-on repairs must have proof the customer was made aware of the repair and be signed by the service manager.

Training

In this chapter we'll examine what programs are in place to attract young people into the business, what type of training is available, and who is responsible.

If you ask high school students if their counselors spoke to them about auto mechanics as a career, the response is usually that the counselor said it was a dirty job. The decline in attendance in automotive courses in community colleges is clear-cut evidence of this attitude. Some have completely closed down their auto departments. Compare this to the parking lots in the 1960s that were alive with hot rods and loud exhausts, and everyone knew what a 327 was or what a Hemi meant. Is that what you see in the high school parking lots today? No. Is that all bad? No. The reason for this is because technology has changed the automobile into a rolling example of advanced and complex electronics. These same advancements have also made all the mechanical parts of the car very reliable. There is now a greater need to encourage kids who are into electronics to get into the automobile business. Conversely, there is still a need for mechanics whose talents are geared (no pun intended) toward mechanical repairs.

Are we as an industry getting this message to the kids? No. So this is an area that requires immediate attention. There are many programs in place once a kid has enrolled in a technical school or community college automotive course. The best programs are offered by the big three manufacturers. Of course that's as it should be, they know the market needs and the school systems a lot better than the imports do. Some of the imports are getting good programs in place and the rest will soon follow. Most of these programs involve the manufacturer taking into their own training center the brightest of the graduating students from the college of technology, trade school, or community college. When they have completed their training there, they are assigned to a dealership anywhere in the United States.

Other manufacturers work with local colleges and dealers so students can work a certain number of days at the dealership and attend classes the rest of the days until course completion.

Another system organized through the dealer associations is a mentor program whereby a student is assigned a mentor mechanic at a dealership. The mentor must attend mentor training, which takes about 15 hours that is normally compensated. This is an excellent program.

Is a mechanic who has completed one of these programs competent to work on any problem your car may have? If the mechanic graduated from one of the manufacturer's programs, he will only need to attend new model training at the manufacturer's school. If the mechanic graduated from a college program, he will now have to attend the mandatory training by the manufacturer of the product sold by the dealership he has chosen to work for. This involves taking and passing an average of eight courses at the manufacturer's training facility; each course is generally two days. The classes are free to the dealer and mechanic but travel, food, and lodging is paid for by the dealer.

Certification

What assurance do customers have that a mechanic is qualified? In the case of mechanics working for a dealer, the factories keep a full history of each mechanic, including training and warranty repair certifications. In most instances, the factories will not process a claim if the mechanic who made the repair is not certified in that area of the car.

Most dealers also at least request, if not require, their mechanics be certified by ASE (National Institute for Automotive Service Excellence). It is even more important if you are having your car serviced at an independent repair facility to look for the ASE symbol, a blue gear with the letters "ASE" in white. Most shops have a large sign on an outside wall near the service entrance and the mechanics wear an arm patch. They sometimes have smaller patches listing the subjects they are certified in just below the ASE symbol.

Who or what is ASE? I will quote directly from their Web page: "ASE is a nonprofit organization established in 1972 by the automotive industry to improve the quality of vehicle repair and service through the voluntary testing and certification of automotive repair technicians."

NATEF (The National Technicians Education Foundation) is a separate nonprofit foundation within the ASE organization. Its primary mission is to improve the quality of automotive technician training programs nationwide through voluntary certification. NATEF is responsible for the program evaluation process and makes recommendations for ASE program certification based on the evaluation. The state departments of education in all 50 states support ASE certification of automotive programs.

According to NATEF's Web page, the motor vehicle repair industry has taken on a new sophistication requiring advanced technical training and computer literacy. The technician of today must have the following skills:

- Thorough knowledge of automotive systems and components
- Computer familiarity
- Excellent communication skills
- Above average mechanical aptitude
- Good reasoning ability
- Ability to read and follow instructions
- Manual dexterity

Summary

How do we attract young people into the auto repair business? It all boils down to respect, pride, and pay. What needs to be done to change things? Let's examine each aspect.

Manufacturers

The first thing the manufacturers have to do is take whatever legal action is required to make the invoice of the car to the dealer a protected document. It must not be available on the Internet, consumer's guides, or to the salespeople. The manufacturer and dealer must set the minimum price that the car can be sold for so the profit is such that the front end (sales) pays at least 50 to 70% of the total expenses of the dealership. This will give the back end (parts and service) the flexibility to increase the mechanic's pay and reduce the price of parts to a competitive level without effecting the labor charge to the customer.

There will always be incentive money from the manufacturers through one program or another that the salespeople can play with to make a deal. Plus there is almost always a trade-in, which gives the salespeople some flexibility. The minimum selling price of the car must be the same everywhere in the United States and the profit should never be less than 10% of the selling price of the car. This 10% should not include accessories, financing, or extended warranties. If all manufacturers and dealers agreed to this, we would be well on our way toward resolving the conditions we have today.

What can the manufacturers do for the back end to make things work better? The primary conflict between the manufacturers and the dealers is generated by warranty policies and procedures. Some if not most of the manufacturers try to work in harmony with the dealers, even to the point of calling the dealer's "partners," which to me is like saying that a mother and daughter or a father and son can be pals. They cannot. They can be friends and mentors, but after all, kids tell their innermost secrets to their pals not to their parents. There needs to be a better working relationship, but the manufacturer will always be the manufacturer and the dealer will always be the dealer. The thing that has to change is the trust factor between the two, starting with their relationship over warranties.

What this means is that the nitpicking and micromanaging over each and every claim must stop. The manufacturer needs to look at what has been paid to a dealer in warranty claims over the previous year or six months. At the start of the next period, the manufacturer sends the dealer a check for that amount. The manufacturer will also select 50 random claims for close audit. If the results of this audit yield, for example, a 5% error factor then the total dollar amount paid to the dealer will be cut by 5%. This will be an ongoing process at the end of each time period.

This brings up two questions: (1) Will the manufacturer stop doing trend analysis? No. Any contract such as this would always allow the manufacturer to monitor trends. If a dealer is making, say 20% higher repairs to front brakes than like-size dealers, the manufacturers have the right to audit all front brake repairs made by that dealer. (2) What if the total dollar amount at the end of the time period is 20% higher than the previous time period? Costs are expected to go up a small amount because of increases in parts prices and labor costs. If the dealer's total costs increase by 20% without a similar increase at like-size dealers (because of a major product problem), they open themselves up to a full-blown audit.

Like any other contract, these are areas that have to be worked out between the dealers and the manufacturers. Yes, I said "between the manufacturer and the dealer," not a contract written by the manufacturer's lawyers and laid in front of the dealer for a signature. Remember all the talk about working closer with the dealers, partners, and so on? Well, it's time to walk the walk. Granted, the arguments over the 50 claims that are audited will be tough, but it is better than the constant arguments that now exist because of micro-management. The dealer would have more freedom but would need to remember that junk (phoney) claims may be among the 50 that are audited. Junk claims could also bump their total claim amount to a level that raises the audit flag, so the controls are still there.

All manufacturers are concerned with reducing warranty costs, but nitpicking the dealers intensifies an already adversarial relationship between the service and warranty departments and has about as much impact on total warranty costs as trying to implode a building with firecrackers. There are three ways to reduce warranty costs: (1) quality of the product, (2) proper training of the mechanics, and (3) foolproof diagnostic equipment.

What other issues do the manufacturers need to address? One is a reward system for CSI scores. If the reward system is to be shared with employees, it must be a signed agreement between the dealer and the manufacturer—not a verbal agreement.

Another part of the CSI surveys that should change is customer surveys being done only on those who have had warranty repairs made within a certain time period. What is the difference between that and random surveys of any repair? First, when a dealer knows the specific customers who will be surveyed, they treat those customers like kings and queens. This isn't right—all customers should be treated that way. Second, if a dealer believes a customer will not give an "excellent" rating, they may eat the claim rather than risk losing points on the survey. They are not only cheating but they are screwing up the warranty statistics.

One of the domestic manufacturers recently came out with a new program to try to get the brake, battery, and shock absorber business back into the dealers rather than the specialty shops. This is a great idea except that the mechanic's flat rate was cut to make the price competitive. I am sure the person who came up with the idea meant well, but how would you like it if every time your boss came up with a special program it cost you money? What do the mechanics think about the program? Their general opinion was that it is about time they called in the union and let them handle it.

Dealers

During a recent visit to a dealer, one of the mechanics called me over to discuss a problem car—or so I thought. He actually wanted a shoulder to cry on. He told me he had worked on an older model car for six hours before he found the problem. The service manager asked him if he would accept four hours because the customer could not afford the bill. The mechanic, one of the best in the shop, worked hard to find and fix the problem, using some of his tools (worth $40,000) and all of his experience (20 years). In what other business could the boss ask you to work for free and get away with it?

Another day I visited a dealer in a Midwest city to help a mechanic solve a problem. This particular mechanic is the only one who works on our product; the other mechanics at the dealer worked on domestics. Before he called me, he spent quite a bit of time trying to solve the problem on his own. Why? Because his pride would not allow him to call until he had exhausted all of the tests he could think of so he wouldn't appear stupid when I got there. (I have known this mechanic for many years and I can assure you he is very bright.)

When we had the problem resolved, he said he was happy the car was fixed, but because of that car and another I had helped him fix over the phone, he would only get paid for 22 hours that week—half of what he had clocked in. Because this kind of thing had been happening more and more, he had turned in his noticed and accepted a job driving a truck, where if he worked 40 hours he would get paid for 40 hours.

Although he didn't say what the new job would pay, I suspect it was substantially more than the $15 an hour the dealer was paying him. He also told me that two of the domestic mechanics were quitting in a few weeks to start their own business fixing suntan equipment. All three of these mechanics are in their forties with at least 20 years of experience each. Who will replace them?

It has to stop. *The flat rate system died many years ago, but no one buried it, so it is still around stinking up the mechanics lives.* What will replace it? Salary is the option I like best but it should be hourly and include good benefits. Salary levels would have to be worked out, but I suggest it be based on what the mechanic earned the previous year less 10%. Why less any percent? Because last year's earnings reflect the mechanic's percent above 100% efficiency. The new pay system will have a bonus that will allow him to earn back that 10% and perhaps more, but don't forget he would have the security of a salary and benefits.

How would the bonus work if the mechanics were salary? The service manager would still track actual time against flat rate time except it would be cumulative for all the mechanics. For instance, if there are 10 mechanics each working a 40-hour week, they should turn out 400 hours. If they turn out 420 hours, they would share a bonus. Say a mechanic's salary is $52,000 a year, which is about $25 an hour. In the scenario I mentioned, each mechanic would get an extra $50. In other words, the shop made 20 extra hours; divide that by 10 mechanics, which is two hours each at $25 an hour. If a different salary base needs to be considered for your area of the country, review the hourly pay for nurses, electricians, and carpenters. For example, in the Chicago area nurses make about $27 per hour (depending on the shift they work), electricians $27 plus, carpenters $27, and plumbers $30.

This system may seem like a good deal for the mechanics, but what about the dealer and the customer? The dealer gets a much more stable staff that will help each other with problem cars. They will also put a lot of peer pressure on the mechanics who are not pulling their weight. Customers get a team to work on their car, which should lead to a much better fixed-right-the-first-time ratio. The good salary and benefits will also make it a lot easier to recruit young people into the business.

I mentioned the mentor system in the chapter about training as being my choice of how to bring young people up in the business. My reasoning for this is because in the not-too-distant future, there will be two types of talent levels required for the industry: the mechanical technician and the electronics technician. Will there be cross-training required? Yes. Each will have to have a better than average working knowledge of the total car. If, for example, a car comes in with the brakes grinding it does not need to go to the electronics technician; it can be assigned directly to a mechanical technician. If the complaint were a drive ability problem, the car would be assigned to the electronics technician. If he found no problem with the electronics, the car would be reassigned to a mechanical technician. In this situation they may have to work together on the problem.

Regardless of which educational system the student is coming from, he needs to spend time with a mentor in whichever career path he has chosen (electronic or mechanical). The length of time spent with a mentor would depend on the program. It may be three or four months if the student is coming from a factory-type program or three years if the student is in a part-work, part-school program.

When I decided to write this book and was in the process of making a lot of notes, I happened to be visiting a dealer in a city that has a dealer association actively promoting the mentor program. A newsletter from the dealer association was lying on the service manager's desk (of course, I asked for a copy of it). In the letter, it said only 50% of the dealers in that city had signed up and the program was now in its third year. I asked the service manager if he planned to participate? He said the general manager would not allow him to. He further explained he had been instructed that any new employee hired in the service department must be able to turn 50 flat rate hours per week. There is no place for a $6 an hour apprentice.

This is shortsighted and refers back to the fact that the sales department must be more of a profit center and cover a much greater percent of the total overhead. This would give the service department more flexibility. This, along with the manufacturers paying a lump sum up front, would free up the receivables and give the service manager the necessary elbowroom to operate. Training expenses could be budgeted for, special tools and equipment could be properly maintained, and the atmosphere in general would be friendlier.

How else can dealers show mechanics the respect they deserve? A comfortable work environment, including a clean, well-lighted shop and tidy break area would be a start. There should also be a room large enough for monthly shop meetings or special training sessions held by the guys from the factory (I had to get that in). What are the consequences of not doing these things? I know of several progressive dealers that are offering mechanics high-paying contracts and even paying their moving expenses.

That is a trend that will continue because there is a shortage of mechanics. Some sources estimate a shortage of 60,000 mechanics per year, based on the combination of those leaving the industry and the lack of new people coming into the industry. I talk to service managers every day who tell me they place an ad in the paper for a mechanic and get no responses.

Often those who do respond aren't qualified or have been fired from every other dealer in town

Last week, while visiting a dealer in a large city that has two of the major European franchises, I was told that the service manager of the one franchise had been fired. When I dug a little deeper, I found out that the reason he was fired was that the shop was backed up on service appointments for at least two weeks. In this case the average cost of the new car is about $55,000. But even if it was $20,000, people don't want to wait two weeks (or even two days) when their car has a problem. The reason for the long waiting time is that there were four empty stalls in the service department that the service manager could not find qualified mechanics to fill. If they offered some great incentives and got mechanics for those slots, it's still only a short term solution. We still have no new blood coming into the system. One technical college in the Midwest told me they have two students enrolled for next year, one male and one female. This is big trouble.

A few months ago on a flight back from Europe, one of my colleagues suggested we make a list of the dealers we called on and rate them based on their current staff. We speculated how many had mechanics who would be capable of diagnosing the cars that will be here in two years. We agreed that only 15 to 20 dealers of the 100 that we reviewed would have a staff of mechanics we would trust to work on these cars. If the situation is not changed very soon, the industry will not attract the new blood it needs and these progressive dealers will have almost all the talented people. There will be some talented people who cannot or will not go to these dealers, but supply and demand will dictate the price a nonprogressive dealer will have to pay those mechanics—and it will not be cheap.

Tomorrow is not too soon to establish a solid pay plan with good benefits. Appropriate presentations could then be made at high schools to encourage students into the industry. But as long as the flat rate system exists, how does a counselor explain to a kid that if he becomes a mechanic he will make about $17 per hour? Or less if he gets stuck on a difficult problem that takes two days to find but the flat rate pays only one hour. Don't forget the fact that $50,000 worth of tools will need to be purchased in order to make him eligible for this abuse. It will not work.

Things need to change and we need to get the word out. We need to meet with legislators to push the issue of raising the two-year or four-year trade programs to the same status level as a college graduate. I recall Governor Tommy Thompson of Wisconsin trying to accomplish this some years ago; it did not work then. But the issue needs to be raised again.

Most of the nonprogressive dealers that are not prepared to treat their mechanics well will likely not be around, because at the rate we are going there will only be enough mechanics available to staff half the dealers currently in business. Perhaps the closed down facilities can be used as satellite test drive areas, because of course by then (around the year 2005) 30 or 40% of car sales will be done on the Internet. These satellite showrooms will only have a few cars in stock for test driving purposes. Rather than a brochure they will send you home with a CD that allows you to figure out what colors and so forth you want on your car, as well as pricing and financing.

Mechanics

How can mechanics ensure their future in the business? The mechanic's most valuable asset is honesty, not only in what a car needs but in not stealing parts that were billed to a customer and never installed. Both of these are intolerable now and will be even less so when the manufacturers and dealers do what they need to do to give mechanics the status and salary they should have.

The next issue is training. All mechanics have to attend the manufacturers training courses and they should all be ASE certified. This is not where it should stop, however. With auto computerization going to the level it is, taking night courses in computers and electronics will make the life of a mechanic easier.

My strategies, of course, are not the only way to resolve current conditions for mechanics. There are a lot of very brilliant men and women at both the manufacturer and the dealer level I hope will get together to help determine a solution. I hope this book is the catalyst they need to get started on these meetings. Whatever the solution, I hope it makes the job of being a mechanic a great-paying one with a bright future and no stigma attached. Only then will it attract the young people we need for the future.